In The Lord's Eyes

Mama's Pearls

Dr. Charlotte Russell Johnson

Author of

A Journey to Hell & Back

Mama Please Tell Me...

Mama, please tell me…
Where does wisdom come from?
Where did I come from?

There is the wisdom that comes from the streets…
It marches to a different drumbeat…
It sets us up for defeat…

There is the wisdom that comes from the world…
It teaches us how to rise above…
It's devoid of any love…

There is the wisdom that comes from the church…
It tells me that I can have so much…
If I continue to search…

There is the wisdom that comes from the grave…
It screams in an angry rage…
"I don't like the wage…
The devil gave!"

There is the wisdom that comes from the Word…
"My words you never heard…"

Now your wisdom I must heed...
If from this bondage, I'm to be freed...

There is the wisdom that comes from Above...
It's filled with so much love...
It came in the form of His dear Son...
He'll forgive everything that I have done...

Mama, please tell me...
Where did life begin?
And do you know where it will end?

There is life that begins in a tube...
But even with that attitude...
There will still be family feuds...

There is life that begins in a dark alley...
These are too numerous to tally...
With his victims, he will never dally...

There is life that begins in the womb...
If death does come...
Life may end in a tomb...

There is life that begins in sin...
It will manifest in the presence of a friend...
It knows its own end...
There is life that begins within...
It says that you can begin again...
This life prepares you for the end...

There is life sent from Above…
It was recognized by a little dove…
It's the consummation of His love…

Mama, please tell me…
How can I find peace?
There is such a struggle inside of me?
Is there the peace that He promised to me?

In His wisdom, He decided to speak to me…
"There is the peace that is absolutely free…"
Jesus said, "It's found in Me!
Choose My wisdom and you will see…
I'll make You what I intended you to be…
You were created in the image of Me…
Sin separated you from Me…
I died to set you free…
New life can begin in Me…
I loved you so much that I died on a tree…
I took your place, so My glory you could see…
You'll find true wisdom when you answer Me…"

Water

By La'Toya Hall

I've seen it all; I've heard it all.

I know-it-all; I've touched it all.

I've traveled the globe; I've been all around.

I can be helpful; I can be hurtful.

I can keep you alive; I can make you die.

I always get used but I have never been hurt.

I can be ice cold; I can stop you like snow.

I flow free like rain; now ask me my name.

Everyone knows me; I know everyone.

I fill the oceans; I am H_2O.

Now that you know, it's time to go.

The cycle continues.

DEDICATION

To *Rosemary and Sam*

My sister and brother who slipped
quietly away…

SPECIAL THANKS TO
Jennifer Smith

For the love and kindness showed towards me and for all the unselfish risks that you took.

Mama Said

PREFACE

"Wisdom is even better when you have money.
Both are a benefit as you go through life.
Wisdom and money can get you almost anything,
but only wisdom can save your life."
Ecclesiastes 7:11-12 NLT

This book is a deviation from those in the *A Journey to Hell and Back* sequence. The books in that series include *A Journey to Hell and Back, The Flip Side, Grace Under Fire: The Journey Never Ends*, and *Mama May I*. My second book, *Daddy's Hugs* was also distinct from the series. For my loyal fans, I will eventually write the next book in that sequence. There are many more stories yet to be told.

In the Lord's Eyes: Mama's Pearls is a tribute to my mother, Evelyn Russell. Many know her affectionately as Mother Russell. Although she has two children by birth, she has claimed numerous others as her spiritual children.

This book is not meant as a praise report of my mother, but rather an exploration of the wisdom that God has graciously imparted to her. It will also include some of her most humorous moments. This book is not biographical. Some names of people and places will be altered or changed.

Solomon pronounces the verdict of "vanity of vanities" upon any philosophy of life which regards human enjoyment and achievements as an ultimate measure of success. Viewing personal gain as the highest goal in life is utter foolishness when compared to the greatest value of all, God Himself. Happiness can never be attained by pursuing it. This pursuit involves the foolishness of self-deification.

Solomon realized that the only way to find true happiness is in the recognition of God Himself as the highest value of all. A meaningful life is the one, which is lived in His service. If the world itself possesses any real significance, it is as a tool for the expression of God's divine wisdom, goodness, and truth. In the end, it is only God's word that endures the test of time. Only God provides lasting value to human life.

I know that, whatsoever God doeth, it shall be for ever: nothing can be put to it, nor any thing taken from it: and God doeth it, that men should fear before Him.
Ecclesiastes 3:14

It is only what God says that has lasting value. Accordingly, we have, *In the Lord's Eyes: Mama's Pearls*.

Introduction From the Heart of Earline

Mama's Pearls is the sixth book in author Charlotte Johnson's series of motivational text. This book is a very poignant chronicle of the faith, wit, and the down-home charm of Dr. Johnson's mother, Evelyn Russell. Loyal fans of Dr. Johnson have already developed a feeling of closeness to her mother, affectionately called "Mother Russell." Throughout Dr. Johnson's books, her mother serves as a spiritual mentor teaching her about love and redemption through her selfless love. Mother Russell loves when it seems that her daughter is beyond change and is unwilling to embrace her mother's instructions.

Mother Russell is a paradox. She is both a spiritually mature student of the Bible, while maintaining her down home folksy charm, sharp tongue, and nostalgic stories of her youth that serve to entertain the reader. These stories offer inspiration, encouragement, hope, and motivation. More importantly, these oral traditions serve as method of handing down the wisdom of times past. A mother's love can be essential to a child's emotional well-being and character development.

Charlotte Johnson shares her mother with the world to offer hope and encouragement in troubled times. This book is excellent for those in need of hope, seeking a miracle, searching for a way to maintain their faith, or looking for an uplifting and humorous book.

Mother Russell grew up in a family where oral storytelling was a method of passing family wisdom and traditions to the younger generations. She passed these stories on to her children. These stories are a combination of Mother Russell's life experiences and oral traditions passed from her father. My heart was touched when Dr. Johnson wrote earlier in her series, "Mama why do you still care?" *Mama's Pearls* answers why a mother still cares when all hope is gone and the world has given up on her child.

As Dr. Johnson explores her family's past in order to bring light and perspective to the present, *Mama's Pearls* is reminiscent of Alex Haley's *Roots*. Dr. Johnson's story is the story of America that each generation learns and passes on. The collective knowledge of the family promotes growth in each subsequent generation. Although an apple doesn't fall far from a tree, it is able to roll downhill away from the foundation. The essential seed from the tree remains in the core of the apple.

This book reminds us to train our children in the way that they should go, so that when they are older, the knowledge will not depart from them, as they choose their own way in the world. *Mama's Pearls* is excellent for every mother, child, friend, individual suffering or in need of encouragement, those who have opened their heart to be a support and resource for others, and those who realize that laughter heals us as a medicine.

IN THE BEGINNING

*Before I formed thee in the belly I knew thee;
and before thou camest forth out of the womb I
sanctified thee, and I ordained thee a prophet
unto the nations. Then said I, Ah, Lord GOD!
behold, I cannot speak: for I am a child. But the
LORD said unto me, Say not, I am a child: for
thou shalt go to all that I shall send thee, and
whatsoever I command thee thou shalt speak.*
Jeremiah 1:5-7

On the cold winter night of November 3, 1939, Evelyn Lavern Alexander was born. She was the eldest child born to Theodore and Earline Alexander. Three other siblings would later follow. Columbus, Georgia is located at the falls of the Chattahoochee River in the western part of the state. It was a mill town in those days. It is here that my mother was born.

It was a time of segregation and civil unrest. It was time when family was considered a valuable commodity. Indeed, it was not uncommon for extended family members to dwell together under one roof. My mother was raised in close proximity of both her grandmother and great-grandmother.

My mother's grandmother was simply referred to as Mae. She was the mother of seven children. My grandmother (Ma'Dear) was her third child. Because of the varying ages of the children, my mother had an aunt and uncle who were very close to her age.

Aunt Bobbie was Mama's youngest aunt. They were more like sisters. During the early years of their lives, they had been raised in the same house or next door to each other. Aunt Bobbie regularly teased Mama about her obsession with neatness. Mama didn't seem to get the joke. Aunt Bobbie was also there during some of the most difficult times in my mother's life.

They attended the public segregated schools in Columbus, Georgia. While attending Marshall Junior High School, Mama met my father, Herman Russell, Jr. At the time, he was enrolled at Spencer High School. They met after a talent show held at Marshall. A short time later, they began dating.

Mama and Aunt Bobbie both graduated from Spencer High School. Aunt Bobbie finished in 1957 and Mama finished in 1958. Mama was a cheerleader at the school. She obtained this status because a merciful teacher recognized that she was just too shy to audition. The teacher simply appointed her to the cheerleading squad. While Mama remains shy to this day, there is also lurking within her is a very quick wit that will escape without warning.

Listen carefully to the thunder of God's
voice as it rolls from His mouth.
Job 37:2 NLT

After high school, my father enlisted in the United States Army. He and my mother married sometime afterward. On Wednesday morning, July 11, 1962, while standing near her bedroom closet,

Mama heard a voice speak. This was the first time that she heard the voice of God speak.

The voice simply asked, "What would you do if Herman died?"

The young wife threw her arms up and waved them towards heaven. "Oh Lord, don't let me even think about that."

The thought of her husband dying was too unbearable. If she thought that she had imagined the voice, one-week later, she knew it had been the voice of God. The next Wednesday morning, her mother rushed to her bedroom with a telegram. Ma'Dear remained at the door, as her daughter read the telegram.

Mama screamed, "Oh Ma'Dear, Herman is dead!"

Ma'Dear responded, "No he's not Evelyn! You must be reading it wrong."

Ma'Dear took the telegram from her daughter's hand. After she finished reading it, they both burst into tears.

At the time of his murder, my father was Airborne and had been stationed at Fort Campbell, Kentucky. Herman Russell, Jr. left his twenty-two-year-old widow and a three-year-old child to mourn his passing. Mama was pregnant with their second child, my sister. My father was the second loss to our immediate family. My mother's father, Theodore Alexander, Sr. had passed about two years earlier.

As Mama sat holding me on her lap at my father's funeral, she felt a shield of protection covering her. She knew God was protecting her and the unborn child that she was carrying, the child her husband would never see. My grandfather had warned my mother, "If you look at a dead person, your baby will be born blind."

Mama didn't tell him, but inwardly, she had her own thoughts, "I don't believe God would let my baby be born blind because I looked at her Daddy."

Now therefore forgive, I pray thee, my sin only this once, and intreat the LORD your God, that he may take away from me this death only
Exodus 10:17

When I learned of the circumstances of my father's death, I couldn't understand how Mama could forgive the person who had single-handedly wrecked my life. Shortly after murdering my father, the young soldier who had taken my father's life wrote my mother a letter apologizing for murdering him. Mama quickly decided to accept his plea for forgiveness.

My sister, Crystal, arrived on schedule. She's never needed glasses. After my father's death, we continued residing in Warren Williams Apartments, a public housing project. This was my mother's choice. For a brief time, we lived in another neighborhood. This housing project represented safety and security to Mama; she had spent most of her life there.

Recently, I had the unction to locate the man who murdered my father. There was nothing that precipitated this idea. One day, as I was working at my office, he suddenly came to my thoughts. My computer was already connected to the Internet. Mama was in the office with me. After asking her three or four questions, I put the information into a search engine. Within five minutes, I heard the voice of the person who had robbed me of Daddy's hugs.

For God is not a God of disorder but of peace.
1 Corinthians 14:33 NLT

Contacting the man who took my father's life was not an encounter that I had planned or thought out. Over the years, I had been filled with questions for this man. Now that I had him on the telephone, I had no questions nor was I expecting answers. After identifying myself to him, he began to talk. On the other hand, should I say that he attempted to explain what had happened? I listened as he talked, not knowing what to say or feel. Mama was in the background. She had plenty to say. She wanted to talk to him. When I handed her the telephone, it sounded like a conversation between old friends. She asked about his children and told him about her children. She told him that she had forgiven him years ago. Still, I listened. I was totally amazed at the woman I call Mama.

Before my daddy died, Mama worked at the Dixie Theatre in downtown Columbus. Sometime after his death, she returned to work there. On the nights when she was working, she would send a cab driver to bring us dinner. This was usually dinner from the Tally-Ho Grill. This was my favorite restaurant. More than anything else, I loved their cornbread sticks. From time to time, when she returned home, she would bring us chicken or scrambled dogs from the Top Hat Cafe.

*And thinkest thou this, O man, that judgest
them which do such things, and doest the
same, that thou shalt escape the judgment
of God? Or despisest thou the riches of His
goodness and forbearance and longsuffering;
not knowing that the goodness of God
leadeth thee to repentance?*
Romans 2:3-4

Occasionally, Mama would have a period of time where she would attend church. Even when she didn't attend, she encouraged us to go. We had our own Bibles and I was always fascinated by the stories contained within.

Over the years, Mama has experienced more than one tragedy. In the midst of each trial, she found a loving comforter was always there for her. She was periodically reminded of how good God had been to her. These thoughts eventually began to swell in her spirit, demanding her attention.

MR. GOODBAR

I will lift up mine eyes unto the hills, from
whence cometh my help. My help cometh
from the LORD, which made heaven and
earth. He will not suffer thy foot to be
moved: He that keepeth thee will not
slumber. Behold, He that keepeth Israel
shall neither slumber nor sleep.
Psalm 121: 1-4

From an early age, Mama has memories of talking to God. My mother's father was a musician. He played the piano with B. B. Toney and The Six Clouds of Joy. The band performed at different nightclubs. When he would return home each night, he would remove all the coins from the pockets of his pants. He would lay them on the top of the chest of drawers.

Remember now thy Creator in the days of
thy youth, while the evil days come not,
nor the years draw nigh, when thou shalt
say, I have no pleasure in them;
Ecclesiastes 12:1

In the mornings, as her father slept, Mama would ease into her parent's bedroom. She was careful not to awaken her father. She would remove fifteen or twenty cents from the coins that he had previously removed from his pockets. She wouldn't take enough for him to miss.

"I am the LORD, and I do not change"
Malachi 3:6 NLT

Mama was in love with this candy bar, a Mr. Goodbar. She would walk to a nearby gas station to purchase her special treat. These walks were special in more than one way. As she walked to the gas station, she would lift her eyes towards heaven. As tears flooded her eyes, she would talk to God.

Mama is no longer in love with a Mr. Goodbar. She still loves spending time with God. God is always there for His children. He is always in the same place. No matter how the world changes, God is the only one who is unchanging and He's totally reliable.

THE MOURNER'S BENCH

Be careful for nothing; but in every thing by prayer and supplication with thanksgiving let your requests be made known unto God.
Philippians 4:6

Prayer is a valuable part of the life of the Christian. The mourner's bench is the doctrine and practice of having the non-Christian "pray through" to obtain salvation. It is called the mourner's bench because the lost (sinners) generally sit on a designated bench in the assembly. The mourner's bench is the place where you mourn over your sins. It is also designated as a place where a loving and forgiving God is able to cleanse you from your sins.

As a young child, Mama and Aunt Bobbie would go to Sunday school and BTU. The overall aim of the BTU (Baptist Training Union) is to train members and leaders in the areas of Stewardship, Baptist Doctrine, and Spiritual Leadership. Additionally, the church would periodically conduct revivals. The week of revival was preceded by a week of prayer.

I went mourning without the sun: I stood up, and I cried in the congregation.
Job 30:28

During one of these meetings, Mama was on the mourner's bench. Mama began to pray and cry out to God. She wanted to be sure that she had received something from Him. In those days, it was referred to as having religion.

We can be confident that He will listen to us
whenever we ask Him for anything in
line with His will.
1 John 5:14 NLT

With the sincerity of a little child, she prayed, "Lord if I have religion wake me up tomorrow at 7:00 in the morning and let me feel the Holy Ghost in my hands."

Years later, the forgotten request was honored. On numerous occasions, God has allowed Mama to feel His presence in her hands.

Today, the doctrine of the Mourner's Bench is almost non-existent in modern churches.

ROLLING EYES

*And dost thou open thine eyes upon such an one,
and bringest me into judgment with thee?
Who can bring a clean thing out
of an unclean? not one.*
Job 14:3-4

Mama has these eyes. They are known by various names. Some people call them dreamy eyes. Some people call them sleepy eyes. Some people call them droopy eyes. Still, others call them bedroom eyes. No matter what you call them, sometimes, these eyes cause problems. Almost without her being conscious of it, Mama's eyes like to communicate unspoken messages. Occasionally, the messages aren't a positive one.

Mama told me that once her eyes really caused her a problem. She was in elementary school. Her teacher's back was facing her. For some forgotten reason, Mama began to roll her eyes at the teacher. When the teacher turned around, she noticed the position of Mama's eyes. They were staring directly at her.

*Let thine eyes look right on, and let thine eyelids
look straight before thee. Ponder the path of
thy feet, and let all thy ways be established.
Turn not to the right hand nor to the left:
remove thy foot from evil.*
Proverbs 4:25-27

Firmly, the elementary school teacher scolded Mama, "Alexander! Stop rolling your eyes!"

There was one slight problem. Mama's eyes began to fill with tears. She tried to bring her eyes down, but they wouldn't move. She had lost control of the movement of her eyes. They were stuck in that position. Eventually, her eyes returned to their normal position.

PLAYING CHURCH

But Jesus called them unto Him, and said,
Suffer little children to come unto Me, and
forbid them not: for of such is the kingdom of
God. Verily I say unto you, Whosoever shall not
receive the kingdom of God as a little child shall
in no wise enter therein.
Matthew 18:16-17

When I was a child, we played very different games from those played today. Perhaps modern technology has eliminated the need for the simpler games, marbles, checkers, hide and go seek, hop scotch, and so the list goes. My favorite game was playing school. During the summer months, while on vacation from school, we pretended to be in school. I was usually the teacher. Usually at the end of an elementary school year, I would ask the teacher to give me some of the textbooks that were being eliminated. Normally, I would help someone who was struggling in school.

My mother enjoyed playing a different game. Her favorite game was playing church. As children, Mama and her aunt were inseparable. When they became adults, the bond between them remained strong. A few years ago, during a moment of reflection between my mother and Aunt Bobbie, they discussed their old childhood games.

Aunt Bobbie offered this observation, "Evelyn perhaps God was in your life all the time. Do you remember when we would play church? Pookie (Catherine Spencer) played with us. There were some other people there, too. We would be in the backyard. You would always be the preacher, and we would be crying."

Mama responded, "I don't know what you were crying about! I didn't know what I was talking about."

My aunt replied, "Yes you did because we went to Sunday school."

"Well, I didn't have to be the preacher all the time," Mama added.

Aunt Bobbie was never one to give in quickly. She responded, "It was just understood that you were the preacher."

Curiously, Mama asked, "Do you know what I was preaching about?"

Aunt Bobbie responded with certainty in her voice, "The same thing you preach about now!"

As if she didn't already know the answer, Mama asked, "And what is that?"

Firmly, Aunt Bobbie replied, "HELL!"

Mama already knew the answer. Over the years, she had pondered that same question. She had always thought the subject of the messages had been *HELL*.

IT WAS BETTY ALL THE TIME

Favour is deceitful, and beauty is vain: but a woman that feareth the LORD, she shall be praised. Give her of the fruit of her hands; and let her own works praise her in the gates.
Proverbs 31:30-31

Mama told me a story of two young women and a young man. One young woman was shy and demure. She carried herself as was appropriate for a young woman of her age, seventeen. For the sake of this story, we will call her, Betty. The other young woman was self-confident and assured. She had a decent figure. There was more of a mature nature about her. We will call her, Carol. The young man was tall and athletic. Let's call him, John. As fate would have it, both women were interested in this young man. Perhaps, he was even dating both of them.

One day, Carol decided it was time for a showdown. She was sure that John would choose her. After all, she had a piece of jewelry that belonged to him. She decided to confront him when a crowd would be present. Somehow, word of the showdown traveled. A number of people were interested in seeing some excitement. When everybody gathered around to see the showdown, somebody was in for a shock. With all three parties assembled, Carol made her move. It was time to set the record straight, thereby proving to everyone that John was her man.

While they behold your chaste conversation

coupled with fear. Whose adorning let it not be
that outward adorning of plaiting the hair, and
of wearing of gold, or of putting on of apparel;
1 Peter 3:2-3

Boldly, she said, "John, who do you want me or Betty?"

Without hesitation, John replied, "It was Betty all the time!"

There was a secret that no else knew. Betty and John were already secretly married. It wasn't long after this confrontation that they were expecting their first child. Perhaps, Betty's inner beauty won the man and kept him. Real beauty comes from the inside. It is not about the outside appearance. We can dress up the outside; but if the inside doesn't match the outside, the beauty is vain.

Mama told me that she wanted to impress a young man in high school. One day, in an effort to look appealing to him, she put makeup on her face. When he saw her, Mama became excited. The excitement was short lived.

After signaling for her to come to him, he said very gently, "Go into the bathroom and wipe that mess off your face."

Mama was so disappointed. He had not been impressed by her effort to dress up the outside.

WHAT DO YOU WANT SOUSE MEAT

*But the tongue can no man tame; it is
an unruly evil, full of deadly poison.*
James 3:8

Now, let me tell you something else about my mother. The quiet, shy Mother Russell also has a very smart mouth. I'm sure that she inherited this from her mother, Ma'Dear. From time to time, Mama's tongue will break loose without warning.

While in high school, Mama had a teacher who had a favorite saying. Whenever she doubted the sincerity of a student, she would respond by saying, "Don't give me that bologna!"

She must have used this expression one time too many in the presence of my mother. One day, after the teacher made her normal statement, Mama's tongue went on autopilot and out came the response that shocked everybody in the class. The outburst even surprised Mama.

Cynically, Mama retorted, "What do you want Souse Meat?"

*"He has removed our rebellious acts as far from
us as the east is from the west"*
Psalm 103:12 NLT

Mama said this smart remark was not something that she had planned to verbalize. She was as shocked as everybody else was in the classroom. She did not intend to be rebellious.

Mama spoke without considering the consequences of her actions. She wasn't proud of her remarks; she was terribly afraid. She was extremely relieved that the other students decided to keep her secret. The teacher never discovered Mama's secret. Mama was thankful.

If we aren't careful, our tongues can cause great damage. Before speaking formally, I prefer to limit idle conversation. It is important for me to speak with a clear heart. Idle conversation can hinder the purity of my thoughts. The audience can say whatever they want to say about me. On the other hand, I have been entrusted with a responsibility that includes treating each of them fairly. If I allow others to feed me innuendos about my audience, it will affect my thoughts. My thoughts will influence what flows from my mouth.

Negative words spoken about us can be a grievous thorn. Whenever possible, it's best not to entertain the messenger. The messenger can cause you more harm than the original message. Second-hand messages are always warped. Occasionally, the messenger has an ulterior motive for repeating the negativity.

They had no desire to stir discord or strife. They chose to be peacemakers by keeping the secret, rather than revealing the source of the hasty comment.

GRANNY, WHY ARE YOU CRYING

For thou hast delivered my soul from
death, mine eyes from tears, and my feet
from falling. I will walk before the LORD
in the land of the living.
Psalm 116:8-9

When Mama was a teenager of about seventeen, she worked to help support the expenses of her senior year. She was happy to be able to assist with these expenses. She earned a humongous salary of ten dollars per week.

My mother and her parents were residing in Warren Williams Apartments. This is a public housing project in Columbus, Georgia. Across the streets from the project was a row of shotgun houses. There was an elderly woman who lived across the street in one of these houses. She was known as Granny. Mama had known her for several years.

One night, as Mama was outside standing near the light pole, she heard the sound of someone crying. When she looked up, she saw Granny. She was sitting on her front porch. Mama walked over to her house.

And when the Lord saw her, He had compassion
on her, and said unto her, Weep not.
Luke 7:13

Compassionately, Mama asked, "Granny, why are you crying?"

Tearfully, she responded, "My daughter is

sick and I want to go see her. I don't have any money to catch the bus. I can't go to see her."

Mama responded, "How much do you need?"

Solemnly, Granny replied, "Three dollars."

Mama left her and went back across the street. She wanted to help Granny. In her parents' bedroom, Mama kept a personal savings account. In the chest of drawer beneath the towels, Mama had hidden her funds. She was saving the money for school clothes. Mama removed three of the eight dollars that were under the towels from the drawer. Each week, she gave her mother two dollars of the ten dollars that she earned for the week.

When Mama returned to Granny's house, she was still sitting on the porch. Mama gave the elderly woman the money that was needed for her trip. It was a gift given from the heart, a gift of love. Mama forgot this act of kindness towards the elderly woman.

In God is my salvation and my glory: the rock of my strength, and my refuge, is in God.
Psalm 62:7

Years later, Mama was reminded of Granny. It was during the time that I was hospitalized at Grady Hospital in Atlanta, Georgia. It had been years since she had thought of the elderly woman. When it was time for me to be released from the hospital, I didn't have a way to come home to Columbus. My mother had a car, but had never driven on the expressway in Columbus, and was even more afraid of the Atlanta traffic. She had probably never driven a car over 30 mph.

My condition prevented me from being able to live alone. All the things that had troubled and depressed me before my hospitalization were currently insignificant. My previous troubles didn't seem important anymore. Before, I had worried about not being able to take care of my daughter. At this point, I couldn't take care of either of us. While I was in the hospital, Mama had placed all my belongings in storage.

Inevitably, it was necessary for me to return to my mother's house, the place that I left at sixteen. Before reaching the age of maturity, I had moved out. My return was totally different from the way I left. I left to be independent. Now, at the age of maturity, twenty-one, I was returning, totally dependent on her. She was glad for me to come home; however, I didn't have a way to get there.

During my weeks in the physical therapy ward, I met a male nurse named Frank. He was one of the angels that God put in my path. One day, he asked me if I had a way to get home. He offered to drive me back to Columbus. This was a tremendous relief to my mother. Her request for

help had been answered before she asked. Knowing her, she wouldn't have asked.

After my first release from the hospital, there were additional trips back to Grady for plastic surgeries. Frank volunteered to bring me home from these trips, too.

Even as I have seen, they that plow iniquity,
and sow wickedness, reap the same.
Job 4:8

It had been years since Mama had thought about Granny. God reminded her of the kindness showed to the elderly woman. After the day Mama gave her the three dollars, she doesn't remember what happened to Granny. God only reminded her that she was reaping what she had sowed. The day that she helped to enable Granny to visit her sick child, Mama had no idea that one day her sick child would need transportation.

It is true that we reap what we sow, whether it is good or evil. Many times, we look for our good deeds to be reciprocated. We look for a return from the person that received kindness from us. This is seldom the way our reward comes.

I'LL MAKE MY HUSBAND'S BANANA PUDDING

She is like the merchants' ships; she bringeth her food from afar. She riseth also while it is yet night, and giveth meat to her household, and a portion to her maidens.
Proverbs 31:14-15

When my parents were first married, Mama was still living with Ma'Dear. Mama's cooking skills were not on the same plateau as they are on today. Ma'Dear often assisted her with cooking for her husband. Ma'Dear also cooked for a nearby restaurant.

Mama was extremely nervous around her husband and this made things harder for her. My father's favorite dessert was banana pudding. During the early stages of my parent's relationship, Ma'Dear made this dessert for him. Mama appreciated Ma'Dear's help, but things had to change.

Mama thought within her, "I'm going to learn to make banana pudding for my own husband!"

She didn't look for a quick fix or an instant pudding. Microwave ovens were not an option. She never considered buying a banana pudding from a bakery or a restaurant. Cooking for her husband was not an imposition. Mama was delighted to perform this task for him. Since that time, Mama has become an outstanding cook. Every now and then, her cooking talents border on perfection.

Mama began teaching me how to cook when I was in the fourth grade. When there were parties at school, I often made dessert for my classmates. By junior high, I could easily prepare a full course meal. I have never learned to cook cornbread to my mother's satisfaction. There is a special way that she likes for it to look. It has to rise in a certain place, forming a slight peak.

When I had my first apartment, my mother came to visit me. I had prepared dinner. The pan of cornbread was sitting on the top of the stove. When Mama saw my cornbread, she didn't even taste it. She threw the cornbread that I made in the garbage can and made me another pan.

Clearly, Mama believes that every woman should cook for her husband. Today, many women would consider that *old school*.

I LOVED HIM SO MUCH

Who shall separate us from the love of Christ? shall tribulation, or distress, or persecution, or famine, or nakedness, or peril, or sword? As it is written, For Thy sake we are killed all the day long; we are accounted as sheep for the slaughter. Nay, in all these things we are more than conquerors through Him that loved us. For I am persuaded, that neither death, nor life, nor angels, nor principalities, nor powers, nor things present, nor things to come, Nor height, nor depth, nor any other creature, shall be able to separate us from the love of God, which is in Christ Jesus our Lord.
Romans 8:35-39

Mama loved my father so much that she wore her hair to suit his taste. It never occurred to her to wear it any other way. She only wanted to look attractive for him. If there was a dress that he liked, she wore the dress two days straight. If that made him happy, it was not an imposition.

Years after my father passed, my mother maintained her wedding dress, his favorite dress, and the dress that I wore to his funeral. The dress that I wore to his funeral is now tarnished and faded. Mama holds onto the things that remind her of a love lost. She also kept duffle bags of letters that he had written her during his military career. Hopefully, she has disposed of these by now.

God can use sorrow in our lives to
help us turn away from sin.
2 Corinthians 7:10 NLT

My mother centered her life around my father's desires. She found her greatest joy in making him happy. Mama planned to spend the rest of her life finding ways to satisfy my father. This was not to be. Shortly after their marriage began, it ended in tragedy. At the age of twenty-two, Mama became a widow.

Although the loss of my father seemed to be unbearable, Mama felt a love greater than her own shielding her from the pain of his death. Over the years, Mama would never forget the love she had for my father or the shield that protected her from his loss.

A JERRY BURGER

And the officers shall speak further unto the people, and they shall say, What man is there that is fearful and fainthearted? let him go and return unto his house, lest his brethren's heart faint as well as his heart.
Deuteronomy 20:8

Shortly after my parents were married, my mother went to visit my father in Kentucky. He was stationed at Fort Campbell. My father met her at the bus station. They stopped by a fast food restaurant for a quick meal. This was the first time that Mama had heard of a Jerry Burger. In this area, we commonly refer to them as Sloppy Joes. My father ordered four of the burgers and two root beers. Mama didn't like the taste of the root beer. She was too ashamed to tell him that she didn't care for the taste. She opted to drink the soda.

The Jerry Burgers presented Mama with another problem. She was too embarrassed in the presence of her husband. Mama couldn't bear the thought of eating in front of him. She had her burgers wrapped to go.

[Your] adorning let it not be that outward adorning of plaiting the hair, and of wearing of gold, or of putting on of apparel; But let it be the hidden man of the heart, in that which is not corruptible, even the ornament of a meek and quiet spirit, which is in the sight of God of great price.
1 Peter 3:3-4

My parents were staying at the guesthouse for the weekend. When they arrived at the guest quarters, there were twin beds in the room. My mother lay down on her bed and turned her face to the wall. My father was unable to see her face. It was only then that she felt comfortable enough to eat her burgers. This was how she managed to eat her first Jerry Burger.

Although Mama acquired a love for the burgers, she never overcame the shyness. She remained uncomfortable when eating in the presence of her husband.

OH WRETCHED MAN...

*O wretched man that I am! who shall deliver me
from the body of this death? I thank God
through Jesus Christ our Lord. So then with
the mind I myself serve the law of God;
but with the flesh the law of sin.*
Romans 7:24-25

Before my first child was born, Mama left her job at the Dixie Theater and began working for the Columbus Housing Authority. It was here that God sewed additional seeds in her heart and ultimately changed her life forever. As a paraprofessional social worker, one of her duties included being in charge of all community activities. This included Bible study provided for the tenants.

Although Mama had never been able to sustain an interest in attending church, she loved Bible study. She loved it so much that when she was supposed to be somewhere else, she found herself slipping to the classes. This was before organizing the Bible studies became one of her responsibilities.

*I recall all you have done, O LORD; I remember
your wonderful deeds of long ago.*
Psalm 77:11

Mama had been thinking about how good God had been to her. She was losing the desire for many things associated with her sinful lifestyle. She wanted to stop doing the things that she was doing; however, she found herself repeating the pattern. It became a vicious cycle. She would vow to stop, find herself repeating the behavior, repent, and the cycle would repeat itself.

Frustrated, one day she told God, "Lord there is no sense in my continuing to ask for Your forgiveness, because I find myself doing the same things over and over again."

There was something lacking in Mama's understanding. She was trying to stop these destructive habits in her own strength. She was trying to accomplish this task without the help of the Lord. Almighty, All-Knowing God understood her heart's desire.

One Friday morning, during the Bible class, the minister taught from the seventh chapter of Romans. As usual, Mama was present. Other tenants were also present.

As he was teaching, Mama screamed out, "That's just the way I am!"

Twice, she screamed this statement. Mama identified with the Apostle Paul. She was doing things that she no longer wanted to do. In this scripture, she also found the answer; she needed God living on the inside of her.

Then shall ye call upon Me, and ye shall go and pray unto Me, and I will hearken unto you. And ye shall seek Me, and find Me, when ye shall search for Me with all your heart. And I will be found of you, saith the LORD:
Jeremiah 29:12-14a

When Mama got home that evening, she knelt at a little red stool located at the foot of her bed. This time, her prayer was different. The conversation with God had lasting results and a far more exceeding reward in glory.

That if thou shalt confess with thy mouth the Lord Jesus, and shalt believe in thine heart that God hath raised Him from the dead, thou shalt be saved. For with the heart man believeth unto righteousness; and with the mouth confession is made unto salvation. For the scripture saith, Whosoever believeth on Him shall not be ashame.
Romans 10:9-11

As Mama prayed with the sincerity of a little child, she wept over her sins. She cried out from the depth of her soul, "Lord forgive me for my sins. Come into my heart; I want to live for You!" God answered her prayer immediately. He came into her life and gave her the power to live for Him.

LORD IS THERE ANYTHING ELSE

*As newborn babes, desire the sincere milk of the
word, that ye may grow thereby: If so be ye
have tasted that the Lord is gracious.*
1 Peter 2:2-3

Now that Mama had found the answer to the
longings of her heart, she had a deep desire to
spend time around others who had found this
blessed hope. Her job provided her with a new
circle of friends. There were a number of people
with whom she could share her faith.

*He that believeth on Me, as the scripture
hath said, out of his belly shall
flow rivers of living water.*
John 7:38

One day, Mama went to visit one of her
friends. After exchanging holy greetings, the friend
requested that she sit down and read something
from the Bible. As Mama sat down, she handed her
the Bible. She instructed her to read a specific
passage from the New Testament. A few minutes
after Mama began to read, her hands began to
shake uncontrollably. Mama attributed the shaking
to nervousness. She tried to control the shaking of
her hands, but the shaking wouldn't stop.

Alarmed, Mama told her friend, "My hands
won't stop shaking!"

Her friend responded calmly, "Keep
reading."

The more Mama read, the more her hands would shake. She became more alarmed.

"I have to go! Something is wrong with me! My hands won't stop shaking," Mama said. She was really concerned.

And suddenly there came a sound from heaven as of a rushing mighty wind, and it filled all the house where they were sitting. And there appeared unto them cloven tongues like as of fire, and it sat upon each of them. And they were all filled with the Holy Ghost, and began to speak with other tongues, as the Spirit gave them utterance.
Acts 2:2-4

Mama stood up and made her way towards the front door. As she cracked the door, strong winds rushed past her, turning her in the opposite direction. Mama found herself going up her friend's steps praising the Lord.

God doesn't have to move when we think He should; nor does He have to move where we think He should. He doesn't have to move the way that we think that He should. He's not limited by our understanding.

ARE YOU CALLING ME

Wherefore the rather, brethren, give diligence to make your calling and election sure: for if ye do these things, ye shall never fall: For so an entrance shall be ministered unto you abundantly into the everlasting kingdom of our Lord and Saviour Jesus Christ.
2 Peter 1:10-11

There came a time in Mama's life when she had a deep feeling that God was calling her to become a missionary. She believed that her work would be overseas. Mama wanted to be certain. She began to pray. On several occasions, Mama asked God if He was calling her to be a missionary.

The answer came in a dream. One night, she dreamed a dream. In this dream as far as Mama could see from the left to the right, there were feet. She was down on her knees with a towel and a basin. The towel was wrapped around her waist. Mama was going from feet to feet washing them. When she awoke, she knew beyond a doubt that God was calling her.

One day, Mama was visiting a local homeless shelter. The feeling came on her strongly. She talked to the director of the shelter about what she was feeling. He shared with her his own calling. His experience was similar to Mama's experience. In the end, he didn't have to travel outside the country. Although he originally thought his mission was abroad, the mission field was at home.

Mama pondered these thoughts. She prayed

for God to give her direction. One day, she dreamed that she was on a street corner witnessing. In the dream, she saw me with her. At the time of the dream, I was in prison serving a fifteen-year sentence.

A fool hath no delight in understanding,
but that his heart may discover itself.
Proverbs 18:2

When Mama shared the dream with me, I had my own thoughts. I didn't tell her, but I had no plans of standing on a street corner. Nevertheless, I was convinced that one day God would use all the madness in my life to help someone else.

Three years later, Mama and I began our jail ministry. This has been expanded to prison ministry. Needless to say, Mama's dream was right; we have been witnesses on more than one street corner.

WHAT KIND OF VESSEL AM I

*Hath not the potter power over the clay, of the
same lump to make one vessel unto honour, and
another unto dishonour*
Romans 9:21

There was a couple in the church that was a
great encouragement to Mama. In our church, it
was customary to have a spiritually minded woman
do the reading for Bible study. This was a five-
minute talk that preceded the actual lesson. The
teacher asked Mama to do the devotional. This was
a big step for my shy mother.

*But be ye doers of the word, and not hearers
only, deceiving your own selves. For if any be a
hearer of the word, and not a doer, he is like
unto a man beholding his natural face in a
glass: For he behold himself, and goeth
his way, and straightway forgetteth what
manner of man he was.*
James 1:22-24

The devotional scriptures were taken from
James. The scripture was about being doers of the
word. Mama carefully prepared for the talk. When
she was finished, the teacher walked over to her.
Before Mama could return to her seat, she reached
her. The teacher was grinning and laughing. She
reached out and embraced Mama.

Astonished, she said, "The very one you
think not! The very one you think not!"

Later, her husband added his comments. He told Mama, "I'm going to ask the pastor if you can speak one night during the revival."

Mama begged the minister, "Please! Don't do that! Please!"

Not long after that, the minister was sitting in the pulpit with the pastor. When Mama looked up at him, he was nodding his head in an up and down motion. She knew that he had carried out his promise. The pastor had agreed to let her speak. Fear gripped Mama's heart.

Know ye not that ye are the temple of God, and that the Spirit of God dwelleth in you? If any man defile the temple of God, him shall God destroy; for the temple of God is holy, which temple ye are.
1 Corinthians 3:16-17

God gave her the title for the message, *What Kind of Vessel am I?* Ironically, Mama felt unworthy to carry the message. She knew that she was not representing herself, but God. Representing God was an awesome responsibility. It still is!

GOD WILL USE ANYBODY WHO'S TOTALLY COMMITTED TO HIM

For Jacob My servant's sake, and Israel Mine elect, I have even called thee by thy name: I have surnamed thee, though thou hast not known Me.
Isaiah 45:4

Mama told me a story about a famous Christian evangelist. She said there was sign that read, "The world has yet to see what God will do with the man or woman who is totally committed to Him." The evangelist responded, "By the grace of God, I'll be that man!"

It's still true! If we are willing to present ourselves as a living sacrifice, God has a place prepared for our service. Mama says that there is a problem with living sacrifices.

She often says, "A living sacrifice just keeps crawling off the altar."

One day, we are committed to God; the next day, we are committed to ourselves. We spend a lot of time telling God what we want. We spend very little time asking Him what He wants from us. We are committed to following Him when all the lights are turned on. When the lights are dim and we can't see our way, we find it hard to follow God. People jump off the altar and attempt to take control of their lives.

But as it is written, Eye hath not seen, nor ear heard, neither have entered into the heart

of man, the things which God hath
prepared for them that love Him.
1 Corinthians 2:9

There is no need to be envious of anyone who is being used by God in any ministry. If anyone will totally submit to God, He is willing to use him or her in His service. God has given all His children spiritual gifts. These gifts are to be used for the glory and upbuilding of His kingdom.

When believers submit to God, He gets the glory for our actions. He's willing if the believer will become willing. He still loves a willing sacrifice. Truly, the world has yet to see what God will do with the man or woman who is totally committed to Him.

IF YOU DON'T CARE WHERE GOD USES YOU

*Look thou upon me, and be merciful unto me, as
Thou usest to do unto those that love Thy name.
Order my steps in Thy word: and let not any
iniquity have dominion over me.*
Psalm 119:132-133

Mama has a saying, "If you don't care where
God uses you, He will always have somewhere to
use you." The harvest is still plentiful. The fields are
still white unto harvest. Most of all, the laborers are
still few. Uncle Sam may still need a few good men,
but Almighty Most Holy God needs willing men and
women.

A few years ago, Mama was involved in a
minor motor vehicular accident. The responding
officer gave her a citation. She was resigned to pay
the citation. When she told me about the situation, I
had other ideas. Knowing that Mama has never
driven over thirty miles per hour, has never parked
close to anyone, or ran a red light; I knew that she
was not at fault.

When she told me the circumstances of the
accident, there was no way I was going to let this
injustice go. To make matters worse, she told me
that the officer was rude to her. It took me several
days to track down the officer's supervisor, but I
was determined that justice would be done. Mama
begged me to take her to pay the ticket. Instead, I
took her straight to the supervisor's office.

Mama was reluctant to tell the supervisor what had happened. She kept saying that she didn't want to get the officer in trouble. The more she hesitated, the more I pushed her to tell the story. Whenever she thinks the old Charlotte is trying to rise up, she has a way of assassinating the pronunciation of my name.

With an exaggerated slur, she pleaded with me, "C-h-a-r-l-o-t-t-e! Let it go!"

Cutting her off, I replied, "No Ma'am!"

This wasn't the first time that she called my name in this manner. I understood what she meant when she called my name that way. It never works to stop me, but she never stops trying. At the end of the meeting, the supervisor apologized for the rude behavior of the officer and advised Mama to go to court on the citation.

Now, by the time the case got to court, Mama was no longer reluctant. The courtroom was full of officers and onlookers. When Mama's case was called, she approached the bench along with the officer. First, he was given a chance to present his case. When Mama got a chance to speak, he probably wished that he had skipped court. Mama never says anything without using her hands. This day would be no different. I leaned forward in my seat to be sure that I heard her every word.

Mama began by explaining that she was traveling down Tenth Avenue heading towards Thirteenth Street. A large SUV was in front of her. With the SUV in the intersection, the light changed to red. Traffic on Thirteenth Street was heavy. The driver unable to see the car behind her backed back. She struck Mama's car. There was no real body damage to either car.

When the police officer arrived, there was only one witness. The woman driving the SUV lied about how the accident happened. When Mama attempted to explain what had happened, the officer interrupted her. It was at this point that Mama told him to ask the only witness.

Mama flung her hands towards heaven, and said, "I told him to ask the Lord what happened!"

From the time that Mama had begun to talk, the officer had dropped his head and kept it there. Now, his peers covered their mouths to hide their laughter. The judge leaned across the bench.

Looking over her glasses, she asked for clarity, "You told him to ask who?"

Mama threw her hands up again, and repeated, "I told him to ask the Lord if he didn't believe me! The woman backed into me!"

By this time, everybody in the courtroom was laughing. The officer kept his head down. In the end, Mama didn't have to pay the ticket. Mama was more excited about having the opportunity to talk about the Lord in the courtroom.

On another occasion, we were having a church fellowship at a local restaurant. We were not eating in a private dining room and people were sitting at the tables around us. Someone asked Mama a question. Right in the middle of the Sunday afternoon rush, Mama got excited and went into a message.

People stopped eating to listen. When she was finished, they returned to eating their food. Mama was unaware that people at the other tables were listening. That is until they started stopping by our table on their way out of the restaurant. They told her that they really enjoyed the message. Then, she was embarrassed.

Warning! Don't do this one unless you are sure that God is leading you. This wasn't planned.

The opportunities to enroll in God's service are vast and numerous. He's already read your resume and has the perfect job opportunity for you. The benefits' package is par echelon. The supervisor has an open door policy. You can begin work immediately.

The steps of a good man are ordered by the LORD: and He delighteth in His way.
Psalm 37:23

So many times, believers decide where they want to be utilized. They decide how they want to be used. They even decide when they want to be used. Some Christian believers decide how much preparation is required before conducting formal ministry. Some even decide that no preparation is necessary.

Today, independent churches are springing up rapidly. Still, there remains a famine in the land for the *word of God*. It has been said that some were called, some were sent, and some just up and went.

And though I have the gift of prophecy, and understand all mysteries, and all knowledge; and though I have all faith, so that I could remove mountains, and have not charity, I am nothing. And though I bestow all my goods to feed the

*poor, and though I give my body to be burned,
and have not charity, it profiteth me nothing.*
1 Corinthians 13:2

Many professing Christians have a desire for the limelight gifts, the flashy gifts, and the showy gifts. Just as God has said that alms (gifts of charity) are to be given in secret, He wants gifts of compassion expressed in secret. Private obedience will also lead to public blessings.

There is still a need for the gifts of help.. There is still a need for deacons. There is still aneed for street evangelism, hospital ministries, nursing home ministries, and youth ministries. These are just a few areas. The need is great. There are those that have been called to fill the need. The sign still reads, "Now Hiring." If you are willing to relocate, He is willing to use you.

WHAT DID HE TAKE WITH HIM

*As he came forth of his mother's womb, naked
shall he return to go as he came, and shall take
nothing of his labour, which he may carry away in
his hand. And this also is a sore evil, that in all
points as he came, so shall he go: and what profit
hath he that hath laboured for the wind? All his
days also he eateth in darkness, and he hath
much sorrow and wrath with his sickness... Every
man also to whom God hath given riches and
wealth, and hath given him power to eat thereof,
and to take his portion, and to rejoice in his
labour; this is the gift of God. For he shall not
much remember the days of his life; because
God answereth him in the joy of his heart.*
Ecclesiastes 5:15-20

A few years ago, Mama and I attended a
funeral. The person who died seemed to have the
finest of this world's goods. During his lifetime, it
seemed that he lacked nothing in material wealth.
Appearances are often misleading or deceiving.

As we were riding along in the funeral
procession, Mama had one of her moments. This
time, it wasn't a dream. She had a moment of
enlightenment.

As the hearse was leading the front of the
procession, God spoke to her. Everything that the
person who had died owned had been left on earth.
There were no treasures awaiting his arrival in
heaven. While he gave thoughts to acquiring

earthly treasures, he gave no thought for the condition of his soul. He gave no thought to preparing for eternity. Everything that he left on earth would soon pass to others.

He that loveth silver shall not be satisfied with silver; nor he that loveth abundance with increase: this is also vanity. When goods increase, they are increased that eat them: and what good is there to the owners thereof, saving the beholding of them with their eyes?
Ecclesiastes 5:10-11 NLT

So many times, our lives are consumed by the troubles that we face each day. We strive for so many things that we presume will bring happiness. On occasion, they bring temporary relief or happiness. True happiness comes from within. If we spend our lives accumulating things, one day they pass to others who will place minimal value on the things that we worked so hard to acquire. Because they have no vested interest in them, they will not hold the value for them that they held for us. Moth and dust will eat up even the things that we value. Only the things that we do for Christ will last.

YOUR PREACHING IS NO GREATER THAN THE LIFE YOU LIVE

Mine heart within me is broken because of the prophets; all my bones shake; I am like a drunken man, and like a man whom wine hath overcome, because of the LORD, and because of the words of his holiness. For the land is full of adulterers; for because of swearing the land mourneth; the pleasant places of the wilderness are dried up, and their course is evil, and their force is not right. For both prophet and priest are profane; yea, in my house have I found their wickedness, saith the LORD.
Jeremiah 23:9-11

Mama says that if our lifestyle doesn't match our preaching, it affects the way our messages will be received. If there is no follow through to the messages that we preach, we make mockery of that very message. We also cause others to blaspheme the name of God. Because our lives are hypocritical, we give others an inaccurate perception of Christianity. Christian still means Christ-like. When we profess the name of Christ, we tell the world, this is what Christ is like. On the other hand, as the famous bracelet says, "This is what Jesus would do."

It has been said that when someone is preaching if you look on the faces of their family members, you will know the sincerity of the messenger. Now, some adults have learned to pretend all is well. In the face of a child, the real truth is manifested.

Mama still remembers the face of one child as she stared at her father. Whenever he was preaching, she would roll her eyes at him. The look on her face told the real truth. His message and his life were at odds.

Some seem to have forgotten that the husbandman is the first partaker of the fruit. This simply means that the message is first directed to the messenger. To him who knows to do good and doeth it not, this is a sin.

A good man out of the good treasure of his heart bringeth forth that which is good; and an evil man out of the evil treasure of his heart bringeth forth that which is evil: for of the abundance of the heart his mouth speaketh.
Luke 6:45

A couple of years ago, I went to speak at a prison. Earline was with me. On the way there, my voice began to leave me. The closer we came to the prison, the worse my voice sounded.

Earline said, "Don't worry Mama, I'll speak for you!"

Knowing that she was bluffing, I said, "Alright!"

As we pulled into parking lot of the prison, Earline said, "By the way, what were you going to speak about?"

Still going with the flow, I replied, "I don't know!"

Her children arise up, and call her blessed;
Proverbs 31:28a

That was the truth; I didn't know. When we got inside, a young man asked me who was going to introduce me. I told him Earline. This was something that she had never done before. There were several hundred inmates present.

With a look of shock on her face, she said, "Mama, what am I supposed to say?"

I simply responded, "Speak from your heart. Tell the truth."

When the program began, a gospel group sang several songs. I still didn't know what my topic was going to be. I didn't tell Earline, but I was more concerned about what she was going to say. I had given her free reign to tell the truth about me. It was too late to take my words back.

I sinned, but it was not worth it. God rescued me from the grave, and now my life is filled with light.
Job 33:27 NLT

This was a very humbling experience. The truth was I haven't always been a good mother. At this moment, I am far from perfect. There is still a lot of room for growth. Truthfully, I didn't know if I was prepared to hear what she had to say. I braced myself for the worse and waited for the truth.

As Earline spoke, she cried. I cried, too. Honestly, I don't know if I cried because my child cried or if I cried in relief. It was probably a little of both. The words that she said are forgotten. What's important is that God allowed me a chance to correct some of the garbage that I showed her.

If your child were asked to speak honestly about your life, what would they say? If people are watching them when we speak, what is shown on their faces? Does the message say, "Fake? Liar? Hypocrite? Abuser? Molester? Thief? Neglector?" Or does it say, "Amen! So be it! Praise God!" How many of us would honestly feel comfortable saying, "May the works that I've done speak for me?"

EVERY DEVIL WORSHIPPER ISN'T WEARING BLACK

They provoked Him to jealousy with strange gods, with abominations provoked they Him to anger. They sacrificed unto devils, not to God; to gods whom they knew not, to new gods that came newly up, whom your fathers feared not.
Deuteronomy 32:16-17

Several years ago, I was training at a clinic. A young man came in for services. Immediately, his appearance drew the attention of everyone present. This was before body piercing became as popular as it is today. His nose, his lip, his eyebrows, his ears, and some other parts were pierced. I know this to be true, because I asked him. He was dressed in all black. His t-shirt and hat were decorated with a skull and bones. There were chains hanging from his clothes.

Although he frequented this clinic often, no one was eager to serve him. Even though I had reservations, I agreed to take on the task. During the whole process, I was praying. Afterward one employee asked me if I knew what he was.

I responded without hesitation, "Of course! He's a devil worshipper."

Thou believest that there is one God; thou doest well: the devils also believe, and tremble. But wilt thou know, O vain man, that faith

without works is dead?
James 2:19-20

A few days later, I was at my home watching television. Several members of my immediate family were present. There was a program on discussing satanic cults. We began talking about the way they dress. Mother Russell was present.

Suddenly, she blurted out, "All devil worshippers aren't wearing black! Anybody who is not serving the Lord is a devil worshipper!"

The blood of Christ will purify our hearts from deeds that lead to death so that we can worship the living God.
Hebrews 9:14 NLT

It is true; we are either for God or against Him. There is no middle ground. Our actions and our lifestyles tell the world who we worship. We worship God or we worship the devil. It doesn't matter what type of clothing we wear. It doesn't matter if our bodies are pierced or not. If we worship Him, we will live a life that brings Him glory.

I'LL NEVER FORGET YOU

Remember the days of old, consider the years of many: ask thy father, and he will shew thee; thy elders, and they will tell thee.
Deuteronomy 32:7

My mother and my granddaughter have a very special relationship. Indeed, every so often, it seems that Toya has found a personal servant in my mother. Like her mother, Toya loves television. On occasion, when she is supposed to be sleeping, she's watching television.

One night, she was watching late night television. It was probably closer to morning. Everybody else was asleep. Toya decided to awaken Mama. She went quietly down the hall to the room where Mama was sleeping. Toya was around three years old at the time.

Toya said in an almost silent whisper, "Granny Eba (mispronouncing Evelyn) wake up!"

A sleepy and concerned grandmother responded, "What is it Toya?"

With a voice that begged for sympathy, she said, "I was watching TV and they showed all this food. Now, I'm hungry."

Wanting to oblige her grandchild, Mama asked, "What do you want child?"

Happily, Toya responded, "A fish sandwich!"

Shocked, Mama replied, "I'm not making you a fish sandwich! Stop watching the TV!"

A surprised Toya pleaded, "But I'm hungry!"

In the end, Toya won. It wasn't a fish sandwich, but Mama did prepare her something to eat.

"Here on earth you will have many trials and sorrows. But take heart, because I have overcome the world."
John 16:33 NLT

Mama and Toya have also shared some very special moments. Several years ago, my mother went through a time where she was extremely mistreated, mostly verbal abuse. She would often come to my home. God used Toya to encourage her. When Mama would arrive, Toya would meet her at the door.

Joyfully, she would exclaim, "Come on in Granny Eba! Come on in!"

Now also when I am old and grayheaded, O God, forsake me not; until I have shewed thy strength unto this generation, and thy power to every one that is to come.
Psalm 71:18

One night, Mama was sleeping in the bed with Toya. As Mama slept, Toya crawled up beside her. She took her small arm and wrapped it around her grandmother. She wanted to share something with Mama.

"Granny Eba, I will never forget you, even if I get old and I get amnesia. And that's when you can't remember anything!"

Mama replied, "Toya that was so beautiful. I'll never forget you either."

Toya responded, "Yeah! And it's true, too."

When Toya was in the sixth grade, Earline took Mama to vote. Mama's voting precinct was at a church in downtown Columbus. After they arrived at the church, Mama proceeded to exit the car. Without asking, Toya jumped out, too. As they made their way towards the registration table, Toya moved ahead of Mama. There were two women seated at the table to provide assistance. Before Mama had the opportunity to speak, Toya spoke.

Pointing at Mama and in a voice of authority, she said, "This is my grandmother. I came to assist her with her voting, because she doesn't have a *clue* what she is supposed to be doing!"

Mama was shocked by what she heard. Not only did Toya raise her voice like an adult, she proceeded to complete the forms provided to her by one woman at the table. When they walked over to the voting booth, the two women stared at Mama. Toya entered her choice for each election. In school, Toya's class had previously discussed the election. Toya was looking for an opportunity to vote in this election. Mama was so embarrassed by the whole incident that she never said a word.

As Mama and Toya left the room, Mama was sure the women at the table were still looking at her. She kept her head down. Toya, on the other hand, was really excited.

Bubbling with exhilaration, she said, "I really enjoyed that! I'm going to be doing this all the time!"

Finally, Mama said, "I don't know who you're going to be doing it with! You won't be doing it with me! Those ladies thought that I was crazy!"

It took some time for Mama to get over her shock. When Mama later arrived at my house, I asked her if she had voted. Again, Miss Toya took control. She jumped in, "You mean, did I vote!"

Earline and I asked Mama why she didn't stop Toya. Mama said that she was just in shock.

It has been proven true, Toya never forgets Mama. Mama never forgets Toya.

TO WHOM MUCH IS GIVEN

*But he that knew not, and did commit things
worthy of stripes, shall be beaten with few
stripes. For unto whomsoever much is given,
of him shall be much required: and to
whom men have committed much,
of him they will ask the more.*
Luke 12:48

It seems that my daughter, Earline, has determined that my granddaughter, La'Toya, will learn the scriptures one way or another. Usually, when teaching Toya a lasting lesson, Earline will quote a scripture. Needless to say, Toya knows some scriptures better than others.

Toya, as she is affectionately known, is a rather challenging child. In many ways, she is unique. She has a personality that is very distinct from most people in our family. She's a very bright and gifted child in more than one way. She also has the wit of her great grandmother (Mama) and great-great grandmother, Ma'Dear.

From the date of her birth, Earline began an active campaign to ensure that her child would have high self-esteem. It was nothing unusual to hear Earline talking to her new baby.

*Thou art fairer than the children of men: grace
is poured into thy lips: therefore God hath
blessed thee for ever.*
Psalm 45:2

With repeated passion, she would say, "Toya you are beautiful! You're smart! People like you!"

Whenever Mama overheard her, she would respond with a message of her own, "You are an anointed missionary for the Lord!" Over the years, these messages continued. They took root in the heart of the child. Toya is extremely self-confident.

Whenever Toya would head off to school, we would say, "Have a good day Toya." She would reply with assurance, "I will!" Toya has never complained of having a bad day. She has never wondered whether people like her. On the other hand, the smart part, well maybe, Earline told her that one time too many. Toya is convinced that she is smart. She values her opinion above everyone else's opinion. If you tell her anything, be prepared to prove it.

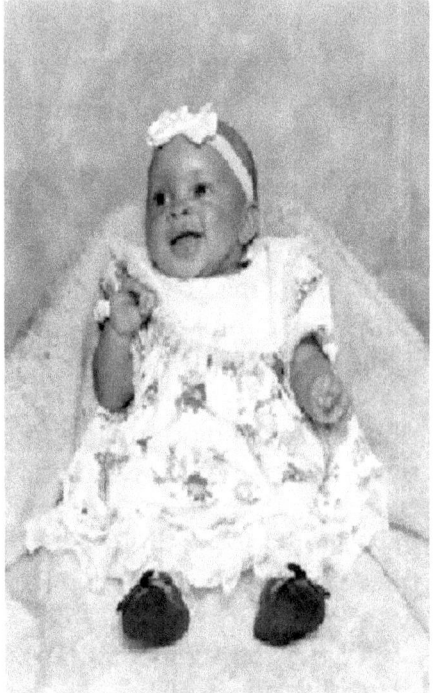

When Toya was in about the fourth grade, she gave Earline a report on her day at school. Earline could hardly believe her ears were working properly.

As if totally disgusted, Toya said, "Things would go so much better if the teacher would only realize that we are smarter than she is!"

She included one of her friends in the smart group. They had previously discussed the teacher's lack of intelligence or the superiority of their own. Earline was livid. She wanted to laugh, but she knew Toya was serious. She had to be careful how she responded. It was time for a life lesson.

Earline snapped at her, "Don't you ever say that again! Don't you even think it!"

Astonished, Toya asked, "Why? We are smarter than she is!"

Toya loves going to church. She has a passion for learning more about God. Most of all, she loves the Lord.

Teach me, and I will hold my tongue: and cause me to understand wherein I have erred. How forcible are right words! but what doth your arguing reprove?
Job 6:24-25

Last Christmas, Toya received an enormous number of gifts. I suggested that she share some of her gifts with someone less fortunate. Normally, she would have been looking for gifts to give away. This time, she hesitated for a second. Earline was standing nearby. It was time for another life lesson.

Earline chimed in, "To whom much is given… what La'Toya?"

Knowing she was expected to finish the verse, Toya quickly responded, "Much is received!"

After Toya said this, she roared in laughter. Mama and I laughed, too. Earline was not amused by this response.

Toya knew that the verse ended, "much is required," but chose to respond in her own way. After all, this was not the first time that she had been asked to quote the verse. Although Toya claimed that she didn't know why she said it, everybody knew that it was Mother Russell speaking through Toya. When she realized Earline wasn't laughing, she correctly quoted the verse. Secretly, she kept laughing.

DON'T PUT ALL YOUR EGGS IN ONE BASKET

"The LORD says, 'I will guide you along the best pathway for your life. I will advise you and watch over you.'"
Psalm 32:8, NLT

One day, Earline and I were working at the office. My granddaughter, Toya, and my mother were also there. My granddaughter and my mother are almost on the same restroom schedule. This day was no different. The doors to the restroom are usually locked. When it was time for their regular break, Earline decided to go with them. Mama walks extremely fast. Earline was walking very slowly.

My granddaughter with her tongue of steel looked back and told her, "Hurry up or we are going to leave you and we have the key!"

Earline dug into her pockets and very calmly retorted back to her smart-mouthed daughter, "Go ahead; I have a key, too. I don't put all my eggs in one basket!"

Well, my mother hearing this knew that she could not let her golden egg be outsmarted and began to think.

Like a flash, Mama replied "No! You put yours in one frying pan!"

After hearing this, my granddaughter began to burst with laughter. Earline was not amused at either of them. To this day if they hear anyone use that expression, they know just what to say.

Blessed are those who trust in the LORD and have made the LORD their hope and confidence. They are like trees planted along a riverbank.
Jeremiah 17:7-8 NLT

At this point, the philosophy that led to Earline's statement is worth exploring. She knows that it is always best to have a backup plan. Every so often, even good intentions go awry. The Lord is the only one who guides our paths and our decisions without faltering.

The Bible teaches us that it's foolish to put our trust in people. People will eventually fail us, but God never fails. Only God is fully trustworthy and fully dependable. We can put all our eggs in His basket.

Contributed by La'Toya Hall

IF YOU ARE GOING TO FOLLOW SOMEBODY

For even hereunto were ye called: because Christ also suffered for us, leaving us an example, that ye should follow His steps: Who did no sin, neither was guile found in His mouth:
1 Peter 2:21-22

Mama wants to be sure that we get our directions straight. To ensure this, she gives us repeated directions. She's not good with a map. Mama only knows one direction to drive to most places.

When Earline was in high school, occasionally, Mama would have to drive her to school. As a teenager, I had attended this same school. Mama had often driven me there. Since Mama was still living in the same apartment, she was well acquainted with the directions from her home to the school.

Driving Earline to school presented Mama with a problem. We lived about seven miles from Mama. We only lived about four miles from Earline's school. Mama was unwilling to learn the new directions. She preferred to drive back to her home and then drive Earline to school. She didn't care about the extra miles. She was more concerned with routine.

Once, Mama got a new job. It was not on one of her familiar routes. I had to ride with her to practice the route that she would drive to work. Mama orally rehearsed the directions.

She repeated, "Red light, turn left."

We practiced several times. In all the years that she worked there, Mama never changed the directions that she drove to work. If I ever needed to locate her in route to or from the job, I knew exactly which direction to take.

When full-service gas stations were becoming a rarity, this presented Mama with a new challenge. The car had to have gas. Mama had never operated a gas pump. She did not intend to acquire this new skill. Again, she opted for the familiar. She drove to my house to get Earline. Although Earline repeatedly tried to teach Mama this simple task, Mama insisted it was not a problem; she preferred to keep things as they were. Nowadays, in spite of all this, Mama gives us directions.

She repeatedly warns, "If you are going to follow someone, you better make sure that they are going in the right direction."

Mama is not referring to a physical destination. She is concerned about the choices that we make in life. Mama prefers that we remain independent thinkers, making choices in line with the word of God.

There are some people who are born leaders. There are others who are content to follow. In observing people, I have noted that one person usually speaks for the group.

The other day, I was particularly impressed with a young woman. She was talking about one of my books. Her friends had no interest in stopping. One of them tried to distract her and get her to move on. She had the ability to think for herself.

Glaring at her friend, she said, "Excuse me! I'm talking! Don't interrupt me!"

The tone of her voice indicated her seriousness. When her friends walked off, she was not disturbed. Before moving on, she finished the conversation.

On numerous occasions, I have heard one person make a decision for the group. Rather than saying, *I*, they will say *we*. They indicate that consensus has been reached among the group members, yet they never asked for input from the group.

When considering the weightier matters of our lives, it is dangerous to allow someone to lead us in the wrong direction. We will ultimately face the consequences of the choices. As Mama says, "If you are going to follow someone, you better make sure that they are going in the right direction."

IF YOU LOSE IT

"God is our refuge and strength, always ready to help in times of trouble"
Psalm 46:1 NLT

Periodically, someone will say, "I have so much going on that I think I'm about to lose my mind!"

Mama has her own version of shock therapy. Whenever she hears someone say, "I think I'm about to lose my mind!" Mama has a quick answer.

With a concerned look on her face, she will respond, "You better be careful! If you lose your mind, there is no guarantee that you will ever get it back!"

Usually, it's hard for them to respond to this statement. It takes time to become accustomed to some of the things that Mama says. The expression on her face can make it harder.

It can become easy to become overwhelmed by the circumstances in our lives. Complaining can be a tempting effort to receive relief; however, this can lead to additional frustrations. If we complain and there is not an obviously sympathetic listener in future recitals, the problem may be magnified. There is major problem developing whenever our problems are exaggerated. We may be unaware of the magnification. Consequently, we believe what was said.

Behold, the eye of the LORD is upon them that fear Him, upon them that hope in His mercy.
Psalm 33:18

God loves us. He doesn't want us to be stressed or burdened by our circumstances. He is willing to bear the load if we ask Him. He wants us to trust in Him as the source of our strength.

Now the God of hope fill you with all joy and peace in believing, that ye may abound in hope, through the power of the Holy Ghost.
Romans 15:13

God is able to turn our sadness into rejoicing. The joy of the Lord is our strength. I have found that whenever I feel overly burden, I need to spend time with God. The greater the burden, the more urgently I need to seek His presence. Nothing is worth our losing our minds. After all, there is no guarantee that we will ever be able to reclaim anything that we lose.

IF YOU COULD DO ANYTHING

*Every way of a man is right in his own eyes: but
the LORD pondereth the hearts. To do justice
and judgment is more acceptable
to the LORD than sacrifice.*
Proverbs 21:2-3

Mama has another saying, "If you could do anything that you want and still go to heaven, heaven would become just like earth. This would mean that Jesus died in vain and He didn't."

At other times, she'll ask a question about a particular scripture. She loves Bible trivia. If you answer the question wrong, she has a comeback line.

With a quirk on her face, she'll say, "Well, the Bible must be wrong then!"

The word Christian originally meant 'to be Christ-like.' Although many dictionaries still define the word this way, the word seems to have taken on a different connotation. Actually, I don't know what the new meaning of the word Christian is. It doesn't mean born again. It doesn't mean "Saved." It doesn't mean that I read the Bible. It doesn't mean that I attend church on a regular basis. It doesn't mean that I have a relationship with Jesus.

It might mean that a bumper sticker is on my car. It could mean that I have a couple of t-shirts with Christian logos. It could even mean that I own a cross that I wear around my neck. Even better, it could mean that I have a collection of angels. I love that Christian music on the crossover charts! Doesn't that make me a Christian? Well, my parents are preachers! I know that counts for something. When I was a child, my parents dedicated me to the Lord. I've always been a Christian. You know, I was baptized when I was only eight. I don't want to go to hell. I've always been a nice person. Surely, that makes me a Christian.

Then Peter said unto them, Repent, and be baptized every one of you in the name of Jesus Christ for the remission of sins, and ye shall receive the gift of the Holy Ghost. For the promise is unto you, and to your children, and to all that are afar off, even as many as the Lord our God shall call. And with many other words did he testify and exhort, saying, Save yourselves from this untoward generation.
Acts 2:38-40

Jesus didn't die in vain. He died a humiliating death on a cross to pay a debt that we would never be able to pay. He died that we might live. He went away to prepare a place that would not be like earth.

No Room for Other Gods

*And it shall come to pass if ye shall hearken
diligently unto My commandments which I
command you this day, to love the LORD
your God, and to serve Him with all
your heart and with all your soul,*
Deuteronomy 11:13

Mama is the Queen of Bible trivia. Years ago, I bought a trivia game. Whenever we played, she would ask the questions and answer them, too. We never stood a chance at winning. There is rarely a day that goes by when she doesn't engage me in a question and answer session. Therefore, when she decided to ask everyone a new question, we were not surprised. Needless to say, no one could answer the question to her satisfaction.

Mama asked, "Do you know why God said, 'You should love Me with all thy heart, and with all thy soul, and with all thy mind, and with all thy strength?'"

We were sitting in my living room. There were several members of my family present. We each tried to answer the question to no avail.

Finally, Mama said, "Do you want to know why God said that? He told me that if we love Him like that there would be no room for any other gods."

*For thou shalt worship no other god: for the
LORD, whose name is Jealous, is a jealous God:*
Exodus 34:14

From time to time, Mama will ask someone this same question. Once, she asked a group of people this question. One of the persons present disagreed with Mama's explanation.

She said, "It not possible to have any other gods. There is only one God!"

Another person in the room replied, "You are one of my gods."

Mama didn't say anything else. She knew the truth. Anything that gets our fondest thoughts is our god. Whatever we spend the most time thinking about is our god. If we love God with all our hearts, all our soul, all our mind, and all our strength, there will be no room for any other gods. There will only be room for THE TRUE AND LIVING GOD!

EVEN IF IT IS ON SALE, YOU STILL HAVE TO PAY FOR IT

And He said also unto His disciples, There was a certain rich man, which had a steward; and the same was accused unto him that he had wasted his goods. And he called him, and said unto him, How is it that I hear this of thee? give an account of thy stewardship; for thou mayest be no longer steward.
Luke 16:1-2

Mama was probably aiming this one directly at me. Although I wasn't present during the original conversation, I'm sure that they were discussing me. Everyone in my family knows that I love a sale. That's probably an understatement.

My problem began at an early age. In junior high school, I fell in love with shopping. After I had my first child, it got worse. Twice a year, one of my favorite local stores would have a big sale. It was called a *Midnight Madness Sale*.

All year, I would watch for these sales. Ma'Dear would allow me to use her charge card. I would repay her later. Sometimes, she would cover part of what I charged. This was because I was shopping for her namesake, Earline. So that we could be in line when the doors opened, Mama would get off from work early. Usually, the sale started around five o'clock. We got in line early. Sometimes, we got in line as early as four o'clock. In order to get the really good deals, I wanted to be the first customer inside the store. Earline would be with us. Oh, how she hated these sales. As soon as the doors opened, she would start complaining.

Earline whined, "I'm tired! I have a headache! I'm going to tell Ma'Dear! You have me out here and I'm sick. Take me back home to Ma'Dear."

Lil' Earline and Ms. Earline

Earline was named after my grandmother, Ma'Dear. Every time that we took her shopping, Earline would complain. If she didn't complain about being tired, it was a headache, or a toothache. If she had to accompany us on these trips, she preferred not to have any new clothes. She was an adult before she got over her hatred of shopping.

Once we were inside the store, I would grab every outfit in Earline's size. That wasn't good enough. I would also get the ones that I thought she would grow into. With both Mama's and my arms full, we headed Earline towards the dressing room. She complained the whole time. People laughed at the complaining child. As we passed her one outfit after another, we laughed, too.

Inevitably, it was bound to happen. There were just too many bargains. Each time, Ma'Dear would give me a limited amount to spend. It was never high enough. Before allowing the cashier to ring my purchases, I had to call Ma'Dear and explain how pretty the outfits were. After all, they were such a bargain. Mama loved this store, too. She would promise Ma'Dear that she would help me pay the bill.

That store no longer exists. Or should I say, it has gone through a number of changes over the years. In the process, they lost me as a customer. Today, it's a different store, but the problem is very much the same.

When my house caught on fire a couple of years ago, I said there were *Just For Me Sales*. This was because everything that I wanted went on sale. Once I picked something out, it would inevitably go on sale.

Earline told me, "I'm going to stop going shopping with you. These sales are just for you; they are not for me."

That was the first time that I ever got tired of shopping! For weeks, I went shopping every day. At times, I went several times in one day. It seemed that I would never get my house back in order.

At the present, I'm trying to kick an old habit. It's a hard habit to break. As Mama said, "Even if it is on sale, you still have to pay for it!"

Mama & her first born

YOU CAN'T GIVE WHAT YOU DON'T HAVE

Keep thy heart with all diligence; for out of it are the issues of life. Put away from thee a froward, and perverse lips put far from thee.
Proverbs 4:23-24

There is a man that my mother once thought highly of. In times past, they had frequently talked about the Lord. Mama thought that, she knew him well from their conversations. She would often tell me about him. She loved his preaching. At this time, I had never met him. Several years later, we both had an opportunity to get to know him more in-depth.

He was often cruel and callous. Mama said that, sometimes, when she walked past him, she could feel his hatred towards her. Mama thought to herself, "Oh! He hates me!"

On the other hand, I tried not to walk past him at all. Mama asked God how this man could be so cruel. God let her know that he didn't have any love. He couldn't give what he didn't have within him. He didn't have love within him and love couldn't be expected to come out of him. We can't give what we don't have.

Live in harmony with each other. Don't try to act important, but enjoy the company of ordinary

people. And don't think you know it all!
Romans 12:16 NLT

At times, responsibility and authority come before we are prepared to walk in that office. In pride, we can become lifted up and exalted. There are times when we just can't handle it. Rather than being humbled by the opportunities that God has given us, we began to think that there is something great about us.

Mama has another saying, "If there is any good in me, it is only because of Christ. It's not because of any great thing that I have done."

Another thing that she told me was, "When I looked at His (Jesus) holiness and looked at myself I felt so unworthy. I told Him, 'Lord, I'm not worthy.'"

While true that we can't give what we don't have, this is no excuse for us to mistreat people. There is one who is able to give us unconditional love. He is willing and able to give us this gift if we only ask Him. When we truly understand the measure of the love that God has given us, we will spread love to others. Before we can love others, we must first receive God's love for ourselves. It's hard to give away something that you don't have. Nevertheless, God wants us to express the same unconditional love that he has shown towards us.

YOU'RE GOING TO GET CAUGHT

*To whom shall I speak, and give warning, that
they may hear? behold, their ear is
uncircumcised, and they cannot hearken:
behold, the word of the LORD is unto them a
reproach; they have no delight in it.*
Jeremiah 6:10

During the *Bonnie and Clyde* period of my life, which could also be termed my *stuck on stupid period*, my relationship with my mother changed. It was at that time that I discovered some new things about her. There were things about her that I just didn't understand. They made me uncomfortable. Actually, I wasn't trying to understand. I just wanted her to stop it. Mama began to call me, warning me to stop the things that I was doing.

Mama has never said anything important only once. If something is really pressing on her mind, she will repeat the message until she gets tired. It doesn't matter if you are tired of hearing it. It doesn't matter if you can finish the story word for word; she's going to finish what she started.

Mama attributed the installation of an automatic account information system by one of our local banks to her efforts. Every weekday morning, Mama would call the bank for an updated account status. Each time that she was asked to provide information to the customer service representative, Mama repeated everything at least twice. They became so familiar with this pattern that without looking up the information, they would respond, "Good morning, Ms. Russell."

The old sinful nature loves to do evil, which is just opposite from what the Holy Spirit wants.
Galatians 5:17 NLT

Charlotte Russell
GWCI Hardwick, GA
1989

Mama told me that God had shown her what I was doing, stealing. That was just the beginning of her dreams about me. They began to come more often and with greater details. As I added new bad habits, Mama had new dreams. She sickened me with her dreams. She was always dreaming something about me. She was always warning me that I was going to be caught. She said the dreams were so real. They were also accurate. I knew the source of her dreams. Despite these facts, I rsented her dreams. She was determined that I was going to heed her warnings. In the coming years, she would warn me of many other things.

Although I am not the only person that she has warned, it seems that I received more than my share of warnings. Sadly, on more than one occasion, I failed to heed these warnings. Because I adamantly rejected the warnings, I suffered the consequences of my actions. In the process, my family got hurt. Some hurts were so deep, that even at this present time, I don't want to deal with them.

Somehow, in our ignorance, we believe that our mistakes only hurt us. We never imagine how much hurt our self-destructive behavior can cause those who love us. When others love us, they suffer with us. They aren't isolated from our struggles. When people are hurting, they may cause intentional or unintentional hurt to others. One, thing for sure, hurt people have the potential to hurt other people.

Wherewithal shall a young man cleanse his way? by taking heed thereto according to Thy word.
Psalm 119:9

Today, I no longer take Mama's words lightly. We have become good friends and companions. For several years, Mama and I went to the local jail ministering to the female inmates. In recent years, she has accompanied me on traditional and nontraditional ministerial assignments. She's still dreaming dreams. She still gives out warnings that warn all who dare to disobey His voice.

HELP LORD

When I looked for good, then evil came
unto me: and when I waited for light,
there came darkness.

Job 30:26

God gave Mama a message, "Help Lord! I'm getting accustomed to the dark. Sin doesn't seem like sin anymore." In saying this, God is not actually referring directly to Mama. He is making direct reference to the church.

There was a time when the church stood for something. It's called holiness and righteousness. The church, school, and government were considered the stabilizing influences on society. Scandals of various magnitudes have all but destroyed the influence of each of them.

Mama heard a radio evangelist say, "In times past, the church wanted the world to be 'Saved.' Now, the world wants the church to be 'Saved.'" SELAH! Meditate on this!

It seems that criticism, scandal, and desperation have caused some churches to lighten their stance. Many churches have become social organizations. They are places that you can go to find an uplifting or motivational message for the week. No longer is the focus on Jesus and the gospel message. The focus is on self and financial wealth.

In an effort to grow megachurches, sin is no longer discussed in some circles. After all, we are only human. We all make mistakes. It really isn't that bad if no one gets hurt. What's wrong with a little fun? God understands. Nobody is perfect. He knows my heart. After all, I'm the king's kid! I deserve the best. I'm still young. I can't be expected to live like the old saints.

What happened to the lights? They have been extinguished so long that we can almost see in the dark. Sin doesn't bother us anymore. We have become tolerant of sin. Help Lord! We are getting accustomed to the dark. Help Lord!

THE GREATEST PREACHING

You who preach that a man should not steal, do you steal? You who say, "Do not commit adultery," do you commit adultery? You who abhor idols, you rob temples? You who your boast in the law, do you dishonor God through breaking the law? For "the name of God is among the Gentiles because of you," as it is written.
Romans 2:21b-24 NKJ

The greatest preaching is not done in the pulpit. When you come out of the pulpit, the real preaching begins. It's not the words that you preach, but the words that you walk that will tell the world what you believe about Jesus.

Recently, I observed a young man selling CDs (compact disks). Another young man asked him what kind of CDs he was selling. The first young man's response shocked me.

Very bluntly, he said, "These are mine. You're into the church. You don't want to hear this!"

This was funny to me. Actually, I asked him to repeat it. I wanted to be sure that I understood what he was implying.

He added, "I hope that he doesn't want to hear this!"

The world knows how the church is supposed to live. The ministers have always been held to higher standard of conduct. Their lives are under constant scrutiny inside and outside of the church. The time has come for the entire body of Christ to step up to a higher standard.

All creation is waiting eagerly for that future day when God will reveal who His children really are.
Romans 8:19 NLT

If we know how the preacher is supposed to live, what does that say about us? Are we exempt from the same standard? Is there one code of conduct for the pastor and another for the people?

Truly, we can all do great preaching. By our very lives, we preach volumes. When no other church member is observing us, we have the greatest opportunity to preach Jesus.

This is a message that God shared with my mother. It is relevant for each of us.

YOU'RE PREACHING RIGHT NOW

Don't let anyone capture you with empty philosophies and high-sounding nonsense that come from human thinking and from the spiritual powers of this world, rather than from Christ. For in Christ lives all the fullness of God in a human body.
Colossians 2:8-9 NLT

A few years ago, my mother and I were fellowshipping with some of the saints. A new pastor was present. We had known him for a number of years. He had recently established his own church. As dinner was concluding, he walked over to our table. After some polite conversation, he invited us to visit his new church. We were more than willing to fellowship with the new church family.

Mama asked, "When do you have services?"

He rattled off the days and times of the services. Most of these days provided a conflict with the scheduled services at our local church. There was only one service that we would be able to attend without missing services at our home churches. Without hesitation, I told him we would be able to attend that service.

He responded, "Another minister will be speaking during those services."

We didn't understand why this would be a problem. My mother and I responded in unison,

"That's fine!"

> *"I am the LORD; that is My name! I will*
> *not give My glory to anyone else, nor*
> *share My praise with carved idols.*
> Isaiah 42:8

It wasn't fine; at least, it wasn't fine with him. The look on his face indicated an unwillingness to accept our answers. He decided to make his request more specific.

He said, "You need to come when I'm speaking!"

He was talking to the wrong person. Mama decided to be just as specific.

With a smirk on her face, she retorted, "Oh! I get it! You don't want us to visit the church; you want us to hear YOU preach! Oh! I got it."

I didn't say anything. The look on her face said there was something she was holding back. After he walked away, she confirmed my thoughts.

Nonchalantly, she said, "He doesn't know that he's preaching right now."

Dear brothers and sisters, I have used Apollos and myself to illustrate what I've been saying. If you pay attention to what I have quoted from the Scriptures, you won't be proud of one of your leaders at the expense of another. For what gives you the right to make such a

judgment? What do you have that God hasn't given you?
And if everything you have is from God, why boast as though it were not a gift?
1 Corinthians 4:6-7

Paul warned the Corinthian church against pride. Paul hoped the Corinthians believers would learn the lesson of humility. All believers should take a position of humility. It is the only acceptable position for a person in relation to God. He is the giver of all gifts. Therefore, He alone is deserving of praise and glory. The Corinthians thought that they had everything that they needed, yet they should have been hungering and thirsting after righteousness.

Preaching the gospel is never to be a personal source of pride. It is a privilege and an honor to be chosen as a servant of God. The gospel message should exalt Christ, not us. The focus should not be on the messenger, but the message. All glory belongs to God and to God alone. He is the central focus of the true church.

With our lives, we tell people what we believe about God. We speak volumes without being aware that others are listening. What messages are we preaching?

No mention shall be made of coral, or of pearls: for the price of wisdom is above rubies. The topaz of Ethiopia shall not equal it, neither shall it be valued with pure gold.

Whence then cometh wisdom? and where is the place of understanding?

Job 28:18-20

HOW GREAT THOU ART

*For Thou art great, and doest wondrous
things: Thou art God alone.*
Psalm 86:10

Mama sleeps with the radio on. As matter of fact, the radio is always on Christian programming. Frequently, more than one radio in the house is on. Several years ago, Mama awoke from her sleep to the sounds of *How Great Thou Art* playing on the radio. Each time that she turned on the radio in her car, the song would be playing again. She even heard the song in a different language. Every so often, it was an instrumental version. This went on for about two months. Mama realized that God was trying to tell her something.

One day, as she was working at a local school, she had occasion to walk down the hall. As she walked, she passed by a man who was unfamiliar to her. When Mama walked out the office, she heard a song playing. She could hardly believe her ears. The sound seemed to be coming from the auditorium. She walked to a place where she would be able to see into the auditorium without being observed. When she looked into the room, she saw the stranger sitting at the piano. He was playing *How Great Thou Art*. This was the only song that he played. When he finished playing, he got up and walked out of the room.

Mama understood what God was putting in her spirit. When we lift man up too high, we attempt to pull God down to a lower level. Mama shared this with a number of people. This message was difficult for one of her friends to accept.

After hearing, what Mama said, she responded, "But we have some really great men in this church."

That didn't shake Mama at all. She was convinced of the message. She was not about to take it back. It didn't matter who refused to accept the message.

Mama reaffirmed, "All I know is what God said. We have placed so much emphasis on man that we have forgotten about God."

"Give honor to the LORD for the glory of His name. Worship the LORD in the splendor of His holiness"
Psalm 29:2 NLT

Oh, Lord! How great **You** are!

I'VE BEEN BETTER TO YOU THAN THAT

Because Thy lovingkindness is better than life, my lips shall praise Thee. Thus will I bless Thee while I live: I will lift up my hands in Thy name. Psalm 63:3-4

Years ago, one of the sisters in the church asked Mama to participate in something she was sponsoring at her home. It never occurred to Mama that she should pray before agreeing to the request. As the date of the event drew near, Mama became increasingly aware that God did not want her to participate in the activity.

Mama was concerned about disappointing her sister in Christ. She thought about how good the woman had been to her. In her mind, she rehearsed the things that the woman had done for her. She had done this for her. She had done that for her. She didn't want to offend the woman. Continuously, Mama tried to rationalize her participation in the event.

God whispered in a sweet soft voice to Mama, "I've been nicer to you than that!"

"The LORD is able to give you much more than this!"
2 Chronicles 25:9 NLT

No matter what anyone had done for her, it paled in comparison to what God had done. He loved her so much that He gave His only begotten son as a ransom for her sins. Greater love has never been shown. No act of kindness could compare to His unconditional love.

Trust in the LORD with all thine heart; and lean not unto thine own understanding. In all thy ways acknowledge Him, and He shall direct thy paths.
Proverbs 3:5-6

Mama decided not to override the voice of God. She called her sister in Christ and informed her that she would not be attending the event. She remained true to her convictions and did not attend the event. She remained friends with her sister in Christ.

GOOD FROM EVIL

Woe unto them that call evil good, and good evil; that put darkness for light, and light for darkness; that put bitter for sweet, and sweet for bitter!
Isaiah 5:20

A number of years ago, one of the men in the church asked Mama to participate in something he was sponsoring. As the date of the program grew near, Mama felt uncomfortable with participating in the program. She didn't want to offend him, but the conviction would not go away. Mama didn't want him to think she was fighting against him. Mama believed participating in the program was inescapable. Against her better judgment, she participated in the program. When God spoke to her, she was left without excuse.

Very gently, He said, "If you don't obey Me, you're going to get in a position where you don't know right from wrong, or good from evil."

Mama repented for her actions. The next time that program was held, she refused to participate.

Harden not your hearts, as in the provocation, in the day of temptation in the wilderness: When your fathers tempted Me, proved Me, and saw My works forty years. Wherefore I was grieved with that generation, and said,

They do alway err in their heart; and they
have not known My ways.
Hebrews 3:8-10

Each time we resist the voice of God, it becomes easier to disobey Him. The first time that we break a civil or moral law, we may be gripped by fear and guilt. Each time that we commit the offense, the fear begins to subside a little more. The guilt tugs at our conscience less. Before long, we take pleasure in the offense. It doesn't seem so wrong. It becomes hard to discern good from evil.

Everybody's not Looking at Jimmy Swaggert

Brethren if a man be overtaken in a fault, ye which are spiritual, restore such an one in the spirit of meekness; considering thyself, lest thou also be tempted. Bear ye one another's burdens, and so fulfil the law of Christ. For if a man think himself to be something, when he is nothing, he deceiveth himself. But let every man prove his own work, and then shall he have rejoicing in himself alone, and not in another.
Galatians 6:1-4

After Mama gave her life to Christ, she constantly listened to Biblical teachings on the radio. Since her childhood, she had watched Billy Graham crusades. She has a few television evangelists who she listens to regularly. Every Sunday before going to church, she would listen to Jimmy Swaggert. On more than one occasion, she arrived at church already excited because of his message.

"Go and make disciples of all the nations, baptizing them in the name of the Father and the Son and the Holy Spirit"
Matthew 28:19 NLT

Mama had witnessed to a lot of people about the goodness of Jesus. There were so many people that she became concerned. She decided to tell the Lord about her concerns.

She told Him earnestly, "Lord, You have blessed me to witness to a lot of people, but I have never seen any of them get 'Saved.'"

If we confess our sins to Him, He is faithful and just to forgive us.
1 John 1:9 NLT

In those days, my children spent a lot of time with my mother. It was during what I term my *Bonnie and Clyde* days. My son Herman was approximately five-years-old. One Sunday morning as they were getting ready for church, Jimmy Swaggert was on television. Mama was walking in and out the room completing her preparations for church.

I will continue this everlasting covenant between us, generation after generation. It will continue between Me and your offspring forever. And I will always be your God and the God of your descendants after you.
Genesis 17:7

As Jimmy Swaggert was making the alter call, Mama walked back into the room. Herman was down on his knees praying. He was kneeling at the same red stool where Mama had been

"Saved." Tears were streaming from his eyes. He was praying so earnestly that he never noticed Mama entering the room. Silently, she left the room. Later, she asked Herman if he had prayed the prayer of repentance. He told her that he had.

My mother responded with exhilaration, "Congratulation son! You're 'Saved!' You're not just my grandson, but my son in the Lord!"

The Lord knoweth them that are his. And, Let every one that nameth the name of Christ depart from iniquity. But in a great house there are not only vessels of gold and of silver, but also of wood and of earth; and some to honour, and some to dishonour.
2 Timothy 2:19b-20

Sometime later, a scandal concerning Jimmy Swaggert became public. It made national news headlines. One of Mama's supervisors heard about it. He knew that Mama was a Christian. He was also a Sunday school teacher. One day in the office, he decided to approach her about the subject.

Looking for some good gossip, he said, "Ms. Russell what do you think about Jimmy Swaggert?"

Mama didn't respond immediately. When he left the office heading for his car, Mama followed him. She stopped him before he reached the car. It wasn't the answer that he was expecting.

Firmly, she asserted, "Everybody's not talking about Jimmy Swaggert! Some people are looking at you and me running to church with the Bible in our hands."

Evasively, he responded, "Ah, Ms. Russell! I'm not talking about that."

It's still true. Everybody's not looking at the failures of television evangelists or political or social leaders. They are looking at their old familiar friends who name the name Christ. They are looking at you and looking at me. What is it that they see?

YOU'VE GOT TO BE ROOTED AND GROUNDED

That He would grant you, according to the riches of His glory, to be strengthened with might by His Spirit in the inner man; That Christ may dwell in your hearts by faith; that ye, being rooted and grounded in love,
Ephesians 3:12-13

Several years ago, my mother told me about a message that she had received from the Lord. It was an alarming message.

"There are going to be some hard days ahead. You will have to be rooted and grounded to be able to stand."

The message was not directed specifically me. It was a global message. Since every word of prophecy spoken from her lips had found fertile ground in the past, I knew these words were true. This was shortly before September 11. Since that time, terrorist destroyed the Twin Towers. Our country has been engaged in numerous military conflicts. Countless companies have closed. Other companies have moved overseas. People have been forced into early retirement.

Gas prices have more than doubled. Many small gas stations have been forced to close. The increases in gas prices have affected every segment of our economy.

Many companies that had been stable for decades have filed for bankruptcy. Still, others have been forced to close their doors forever. Many companies have become desperate for survival. They have developed extreme financial practices. In many companies, customer service has become a thing of the past.

There have been natural disasters around the world. Hurricanes and tornados have caused severe damage. Thousands of people have lost their lives.

Later Mama spoke another word, "The whole world is in turmoil."

We began to meet people everywhere who were in crisis. As the years have passed, we have met an increasing number of people in crisis. Some of them have become so overwhelmed by their circumstances that they see no hope of recovery. There have been times when I have attempted to encourage someone. On multiple occasions, the person responded that there was no hope of things getting better.

For those of us who have a relationship with God, there is hope. Our hope is in Him. He cares. He is rock of our salvation. He's steady under pressure. He is a sure foundation. We can wrap our hope and trust around Him. We can rest assured that all things are working together for our good. If we are rooted and grounded in Him, nothing can shake our hope for a brighter tomorrow.

ONE MOMENT IN PARADISE WILL PAY FOR IT ALL

"Even though the fig trees have no blossoms, and there are no grapes on the vines; even though the olive crop fails, and the fields lie empty and barren; even though the flocks die in the fields, and the cattle barns are empty, yet I will rejoice in the LORD! I will be joyful in the God of my salvation."
Habakkuk 3:17-18 NLT

There was a woman who was going through a difficult trial. She was a Christian. There was another woman who was in a position to help her. Rather than responding with compassion, she asked her a question.

Cynically, she asked, "Why is it that people in your religion have so many problems?"

With a confident response, the first woman replied, "One moment in paradise will pay for it all!"

She responded without a moment of hesitation or regret. The second woman was left without a response. As you might imagine, the second woman was not a Christian.

He that hath an ear, let him hear what the Spirit saith unto the churches; To him that overcometh will I give to eat of the tree of life, which is in the midst

of the paradise of God.
Revelation 2:7

There is more to life than just acquiring things or possessions. The most important things in life are not things. True happiness isn't found in material possessions or wealth. God's love brings joy that no amount of things can give. An abundant life is a quality-filled life characterized by order, peace, and wholeness.

Now the God of hope fill you with all joy and peace in believing, that ye may abound in hope, through the power of the Holy Ghost.
Romans 15:13

In this life, we will have problems. The believer in Christ has the confident assurance of knowing that in the midst of every storm, the one who has the power to calm the storm is with them. To those who endure to the end, Jesus has promised a place in paradise.

HOW WOULD THE WORLD BE

And the Lord make you to increase and abound in love one toward another, and toward all men, even as we do toward you: To the end He may stablish your hearts unblameable in holiness before God, even our Father, at the coming of our Lord Jesus Christ with all His saints.
1 Thessalonians 3:12-13

One day, mama asked God a question. She asked Him, "What would the world be like if everyone loved one another?"

The intense affection and enduring vow made when we accepted Christ, as our savior should be expressed in our relationships with our spiritual family as well. We are expected to love our brothers and sisters of faith, with the same love and respect that we have our natural brothers and sisters. Brotherly compassion and affection are characteristic of the love family members have for each other.

As believers in Jesus Christ, we need to make our love apparent. We should be willing to make an unequivocal commitment to loving our natural and spiritual family. Our love should be expressed by our actions and deeds.

Love each other with genuine affection, and take delight in honoring each other.
Romans 12:10 NLT

Jesus declares that by our love the entire world will judge whether we are genuine believers. Based on our expressions of love for fellow believers, the world can determine the sincerity of our faith. Love is the identifying mark of the followers of Jesus Christ. We forfeit our right to represent Jesus Christ to the world, anytime we fail to show love towards fellow believers. Because the world is observing our witness, we should be careful of the image that we present.

The world is disgusted by false doctrine, hierocracy, and phony theology. They automatically understand love in action. Sinners look at Christians before they look at their doctrine. They form opinions about our savior, our church, our religion, and other Christians when they see how we conduct ourselves. If they see genuine concern and compassion, they will listen to our messages. If what they observe are confusion and discord, we have a hindering effect in their lives.

YOU BE ONE

Then Agrippa said unto Paul, Almost thou persuadest me to be a Christian. And Paul said, I would to God, that not only thou, but also all that hear me this day, were both almost, and altogether such as I am, except these bonds.
Acts 26:28-29

Years ago, a woman told Mama, "Ain't nobody going to heaven, because ain't nobody living right!"

Mama replied, "Somebody's going, because it's in the Bible! Somebody is crying out to God right now."

Sure of her statement, the woman added, "Well, it must be somebody who died a long time ago!"

Mama responded instantly, "Somebody's going, because it's in the Bible!"

The woman continued to insist that no one was going to heaven, because no one was living right.

Finally, Mama asked her, "Do you want to know how you can know somebody is living right?"

The woman replied, "Yes!"

Mama asked her again, "Are you sure that you want to know?"

Again, the woman responded, "Yes!"

"For to me, living is for Christ, and dying

is even better"
Philippians 1:21, NLT

Firmly, Mama said, "You live right! You be one! That's how you can really know that somebody is going to heaven."

So many times our attention is focused on what others are doing. This is merely a trick to hinder us from making corrections in our own behavior. When we measure ourselves against others, we often use a faulty measure. Hence, we draw inaccurate conclusion. Jesus is the plumb line. He is the only accurate weight. When we measure ourselves against Him, we all come up lacking.

Let another man praise thee, and not thine own mouth; a stranger, and not thine own lips.
Proverbs 27:2

Mama often says, "Self-praise isn't worth ten cents."

One of our former pastor's would say, "Talk is cheap, but it takes money to buy land."

When we lift ourselves up, we invite others to inspect our lives. Rather than focusing on the failures or successes of others, we should focus on the example of Jesus. When looking for someone living right, the first stop should be with us. We should be the one!

WHO TOLD YOU THAT YOU WERE GOING TO GET OLD

But God said unto him, Thou fool, this night thy soul shall be required of thee: then whose shall those things be, which thou hast provided?
Luke 12:20

One day, Mama was talking to a young woman about the Lord. After an extended period of conversation, it became obvious that she was not receptive to what Mama was saying.

Looking for a route of escape, she asked, "Ms. Russell, how old were you when you were 'Saved?'"

Without hesitation, Mama replied, "In my thirties!"

Defiantly, she answered, "Maybe when I get that old, I'll give my life to Christ!"

Not willing to accept this excuse, Mama asked, "Who told you that you were going to live to get that old?"

But as many as received Him, to them gave He power to become the sons of God, even to them that believe on His name: Which were born, not of blood, nor of the will of the flesh, nor of the will of man, but of God.
John 1:12-13

The young woman was approximately eighteen-years-old. She looked at Mama in shock. This was something that she had never considered. She was not prepared to respond.

In the early hours of the morning, there was another young woman that became sick. She was taken to the hospital. Later that day she died. It was sad and tragic day for those who loved her. One person continuously focused on her age.

Repeatedly, he said, "But she was only eighteen-years-old!"

I listen carefully to what God the LORD is saying, for He speaks peace to His faithful people. But let them not return to their foolish ways. Surely His salvation is near to those who fear Him, so our land will be filled with His glory.
Psalm 85:8-9 NLT

Our loving heavenly Father is not willing that any should perish, but that all should come to the saving knowledge of Him. No man knows the hour, the minute, or the second that will be his last opportunity to accept Christ. It behooves us to be ready at any age.

BE CAREFUL WHO YOU OVERLOOK

Thou shalt not wrest judgment; thou shalt not respect persons, neither take a gift: for a gift doth blind the eyes of the wise, and pervert the words of the righteous.
Deuteronomy 16:19

My mother has a number of sons in the faith. She has two young men that have been close to her heart for a number of years. Mama has had dreams about both of them. At the time of the dreams, they were both deacons.

In one of the dreams, Mama was walking through the church with one of her sons. As they walked up and down the aisle, Mama was giving him instructions.

But the LORD said unto Samuel, Look not on his countenance, or on the height of his stature; because I have refused him: for the LORD seeth not as man seeth; for man looketh on the outward appearance, but the LORD looketh on the heart.
1 Samuel 16:7

With a mother's compassion, she said, "Be careful who you overlook. If you start overlooking people, you are going to overlook the wrong one."

Mama shared her dream with him. Since that time, this young man has become a pastor. He has a gentle and humble spirit.

Humble yourselves therefore under the mighty hand of God, that he may exalt you in due time.
1 Peter 5:6

Sadly, we often make the mistake of judging people by what we see. Economic or social status often determines how we treat people. Even sadder, at times, we reject people based on the opinion of others.

Several years ago, I was receiving public assistance. This was before I left the street life alone and finished college. During that time, I received food stamps and other subsidies.

After college, I went to work for more than one agency where I had previously been a client. One of my old caseworkers interviewed with me for a job. If he had been hired, I would have been his supervisor. Our previous relationship did not preclude his hiring.

I share this only to say that he could have labeled me as any one of the stereotypes that are associated with people who draw public assistance. He could have called me lazy, stupid, uneducated, unmotivated, a low achiever, trailer trash, and worthless. I was living in a trailer at the time. Again, I'm not accusing him of anything close to discrimination. I doubt that he assumed that one day our roles would reverse. He had interviewed me a number of times. As I sat across from him conducting his interview, I doubt that he remembered me as his former client.

We only know in part. We only see in part. Often, we miss the purpose and destiny that God has placed within people. When we have respect for only certain people, we make dangerous assumption.

Mama says, "You never know who you will need."

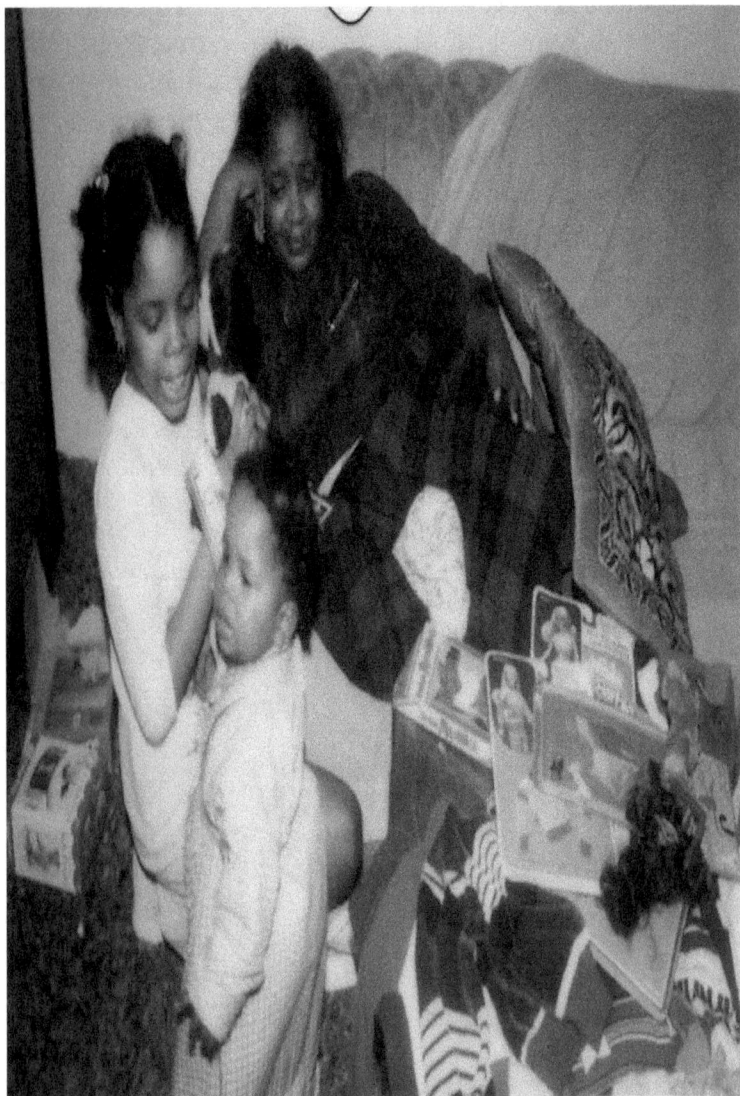

Earline, Herman, & Mama

I DON'T CARE WHAT THEY SAY ABOUT ME

But shun profane and vain babblings: for they will increase unto more ungodliness.
2 Timothy 2:16

One night, Mama was walking home from church with a friend. This was their usual tradition. They both lived within walking distance of the church. As they were walking, they began a conversation. They stopped near a telegram pole. They were discussing people speaking negatively about you.

With a slight attitude, Mama said, "I don't care what anybody says about me!"

When Mama said this, she believed that she was totally justified in making this statement. When the conversation ended, Mama's friend turned to go home. Mama went on to her apartment.

If you ignore criticism, you will end in poverty and disgrace; if you accept criticism, you will be honored.
Proverbs 13:18 NLT

As Mama walked, God let her know that she was wrong. As a Christian, she was no longer representing herself. She was representing Him. If anything negative was said about her, she should examine herself. She should search herself. She was to be certain that the negative comments were untrue. If the comments were true, she should care. If the negative remarks were true, she should repent. As a representative of Christ, she needed to live a life that would bring glory to His name, not shame or dishonor.

After Mama entered her apartment, she immediately called her friend. She told her that she had been wrong. Mama shared with her what God had laid upon her heart; we should be concerned about what people say about us. As one pastor often said, "People may paint your name on a signpost, but don't you furnish the paint." Shun the very appearance of evil. Let your integrity be sound and above reproach that if people say negative things about, no one will believe them.

I see one pastor frequently. His wife is always nearby. From time to time, she waits in the car. I've never heard anyone say anything negative about him. If ever heard anyone say that he was unfaithful to his wife, I would seriously doubt the accuracy of the information.

STICK AROUND ME LONG ENOUGH

Beware lest any man spoil you through philosophy and vain deceit, after the tradition of men, after the rudiments of the world, and not after Christ. Colossians 2:8

Mama got this saying from an old woman that she would visit. The woman would often say, "Stick around me long enough, you'll know me." She also said, "It takes about six months to know someone."

In recent years, I have found these sayings to be painfully true. It takes times to know people. When a person is a consummate liar or great pretender, it is impossible to get to know them. Recently, I found out the person that I thought I knew best was a total stranger to me. Sometimes, six months or six years is not enough time to know someone. What does it really mean to know someone? It's more than just recognizing their first name.

In recent years, I have attended a number of funerals. Occasionally, the remarks made about the deceased remind me of *America's Funniest Videos*. There is something almost magical about a funeral. It makes people with the best intentions LIE. If the person in the casket woke up, they would wonder whose funeral they were attending. They definitely wouldn't recognize it as their own. I attended one funeral where nothing was said personally about the deceased. At another funeral, most of the people present knew the deceased better than the person giving the eulogy. When the eulogist began to explain the character of the deceased, I realized the people speaking at the funeral didn't know the deceased person.

It was only at that moment that I had a new revelation. Spending a couple of hours, a week with a person is not enough time to know them. It is particularly difficult in a formal atmosphere.

I have one request for my funeral - the truth, please. My life will have already spoken for me. I often joke that if anyone lies about me at my funeral, I'm going to get up.

There is something about death that causes people to become overly concerned about the dearly departed's final home. The concern isn't strong enough for them to give their lives to Christ. There is just a deep desire for a quick fix. Even if it's against the deceased person's will, they want the deceased person's final resting place to be in heaven.

Sad to say, not everyone would enjoy heaven. I don't like okra. I've never tasted it; however, I don't like the way that okra looks. After I'm dead, I still won't like okra. Some people hate the idea of talking about God. They hate being around Christians. They wouldn't be caught dead inside of a church. What would make them enjoy heaven? After careful analysis, I'm convinced that it's not heaven that many people desire; it's hell that they fear.

IS THE CHURCH GROWING

And as they went through the cities, they
delivered them the decrees for to keep,
that were ordained of the apostles and
elders which were at Jerusalem. And so
were the churches established in the
faith, and increased in number daily.
Acts 16:4-5

Christ will only acknowledge that which He builds. If the church is to grow according to the word, believers must have a personal confrontation with the living Christ. They must have a personal revelation of the Lord Jesus. They must be a personal acknowledgment of His atoning blood. They must make a public confession of His saving grace. People cannot be built into the church until they have confessed the Christ.

The people that walked in darkness have seen
a great light: they that dwell in the land of
the shadow of death, upon them hath
the light shined.
Isaiah 9:2

Mama says that in the world today, a little light won't do. You have to be really different to make an impact on the darkness. The world has seen so much hypocrisy that skepticism has become the normal response in most circumstances. Hypocrisy exists outside of the church; however, the church usually receives the brunt of the criticism.

Now I beseech you, brethren, by the name of our Lord Jesus Christ, that ye all speak the same thing, and that there be no divisions among you; but that ye be perfectly joined together in the same mind and in the same judgment.
1 Corinthians 1:10

Whenever one Christian falls or fails to uphold Godly standards the entire body of Christ suffers. Each member of the body has the potential to help or hurt the body. Because so much damage has been done to the body, a great healing is needed. People have to see a great difference in our lifestyle. Our lifestyle has to line up with the word of God. The church may boast that they have thousands of members, but if the word of God is not being exalted, it is not growing according to the word.

SEE SOMEBODY CARES

*But He, being full of compassion, forgave their
iniquity, and destroyed them not: yea, many
a time turned He His anger away, and did
not stir up all His wrath. For He remembered
that they were but flesh; a wind that
passeth away, and cometh not again.*
Psalm 78:38-39

One day, Mama went to bed discouraged over something that had happened in our family. She was crying and crying out to God. In the midst of her heartache, she felt alone.

She complained, "Lord, it seems nobody cares!"

That night, Mama had a dream. In the dream, she was standing on a tall ladder. She was standing two or three steps from the top of the ladder. The ladder was in a pretty green field. In the dream, no houses or people were present. The ladder wasn't propped against anything. It wasn't touching the ground. Mama was afraid that she was going to fall. All of a sudden, standing at the bottom of the ladder, a man appeared.

Patiently, he asked Mama, "What's wrong?"

Mama replied, "I'm scared that I am going to fall."

Better to be patient than powerful; better to

have self-control than to conquer a city.
Proverbs 16:32 NLT

The man in the dream took the ladder and let it down gently and patiently. He was careful not to let her fall. She could fill the love and tenderness. There was so much concern. He let her down to the ground. The moment that she stepped on the ground, she heard a voice.

The voice said, "See! Somebody cares!"

That was the end of Mama's dream. She knew that God cares. Mama has never had a reason to feel alone or abandoned again. Since that night, she has never wondered if anybody cared.

God cares for each of us. In the times when we feel all alone, God is there. He is waiting to dry the tears that flow from our eyes. He's waiting to bring comfort to our troubled hearts.

MORE PEOPLE CARE THAN YOU THINK

*Thus speaketh the LORD of hosts, saying,
Execute true judgment, and shew mercy and
compassions every man to his brother: And
oppress not the widow, nor the fatherless, the
stranger, nor the poor; and let none of you
imagine evil against his brother in your heart.*
Zechariah 7:9:10

One night, Mama's back porch light went out. A friend of hers changed the light bulb for her. One of her neighbors was watching the stranger. She called the police. Mama was surprised when the police knocked on her door. God impressed in Mama's spirit that more people care about her than she thought. Immediately, the message began to manifest. Random acts of kindness towards her became routine. God blessed her with wonderful friends and many spiritual children.

Periodically, the lens from Mama's eyeglasses would fall out. Mama was procrastinating in making an appointment with the eye doctor. One of the sisters at the church decided it was time to fix the problem. She made an appointment with her eye doctor. She told Mama what day was scheduled for the appointment. At church, she gave Mama an envelope. Enclosed within the envelope was the money for the eye examination. She went a step further and called the optometrist. She told them not to allow Mama to get any old-fashioned eyeglasses. Mama picked out those exact kinds. They were old plastic frames. The woman that assisted Mama told her about the telephone call. After the appointment, the young woman went to the optometrist and paid for the glasses.

Shortly after this time, Mama heard a knock at her back door; it was the same young woman. She was carrying a beautiful white suit. Another night at church, she slipped Mama some money.

On Sundays after church, we often went out to eat at a restaurant. Several members of our local church would go out together. We would eat and fellowship until time to return to church for Sunday evening worship. For most of my life, I never drank water. When I decided to make this a part of my regular routine, I decided that everybody in my family would also drink water. One way to assure this was during the times when we eat out as a family. Since I usually treat my family, I made a stipulation. If I was paying for the meal, everybody had to drink water. Mama is not partial to water. The look on her face as we ordered would make this apparent. One sister at our church was determined that Mama did not have to drink water.

She would tell Mama firmly, "Get what you want mother! Nobody's thinking about O' Charlotte! You get what you want! Don't worry about how much it cost! Go ahead get what you want mother!"

Every time that we went out to eat, she would say the same thing. She would back her statement up by paying for Mama's meals and beverages. Each time, she would laugh at me.

Once when we were eating out, I insisted on everybody drinking water. Earline, Toya, and Mama were with me. Earline would usually pay for her own drink. This time, Miss La'Toya had money. When I put the order in for the water, she spoke up.

Pointing to my mother, she instructed the waitress, "Bring her an unsweetened tea."

Mama interrupted, "No Toya!"

Toya insisted, "Bring her an unsweetened tea! I'm paying for it!"

Mama tried again, "No Toya! Keep your money!"

Even more insistent, she replied, "I said that I was paying for it!"

We are grateful for all of Mama's children. We are thankful for all the acts of kindness showed towards her. Some of the children have moved away. Nevertheless, they have never moved from her heart or been forgotten.

One night, I was in a store shopping. A man was in the store shopping in a nearby department. He was looking at a piece of crystal. I recognized him as someone who had owned one of Mama's favorite stores. Several months before, the store had closed permanently. When I spoke to him, he asked about Mama. Afterward he disappeared with the crystal vase, heading towards the checkout counter. Within a few minutes, he returned with a card in his hand.

He said, "Give this to your mother; so, the next time, she can come shopping with you."

It was a gift card. This was not the first time that he had shown kindness to Mama. Each time that he saw her, he showed kindness. Shortly after he met Mama, he saw her looking at an exquisite item in his store. He told her to take it home and she could pay him later. When the store closed, he gave Mama several gifts. Once when Mama wasn't home, he left her a Christmas present in the door of her apartment. Upon her return, she discovered a note and the gift.

When we were children, Mama would give us birthday parties. Oh, how I hated those parties! My sister's birthday and my birthday are five days apart. As children, our parties were always held together. Mama wanted everyone to feel free to attend. She made a stipulation that I hated. No one was allowed to bring a present. She invited family, friends, and enemies. We never got one birthday present. She didn't want anyone to stay away, because they didn't have the money for a present.

The acts of kindness towards Mama have been numerous. Kindness came from various sources in unexpected ways. Kindness even came from strangers. Mama never solicited anything from anyone. It is difficult for Mama to allow others to give to her. She prefers to give to others. God decided that she would be a recipient. He wanted her to know that more people cared about her than she thought.

IT'S BETTER TO BE ALONE

But now I have written unto you not to keep company if any man that is called a brother be a fornicator, or covetous, or an idolater, or a railer, or a drunkard, or an extortioner; with such an one no not to eat.
1 Corinthians 5:11

Mama's father would frequently give her instructions. He was not a student of the Bible; however, he shared with her the lessons that he had learned in life.

He instructed, "It's better to be alone than in bad company."

It is difficult for most of us to accept negative evaluations. We want others to think well of us. We don't like to be judged. In most instances, we will attempt to defend ourselves.

Solitary confinement is used as a form of punishment. It can be detrimental to a person's mental well-being if it lasts for an extended period of time. Therefore, most people choose to avoid the negative stigma associated with being alone.

There are those who say, "Birds of a feather flock together."

A Russian proverb says, "Tell me who's your friend and I'll tell you who you are."

A German Proverb says it best, "When a dove begins to associate with crows its feathers remain white but its heart grows black."

I once heard someone say, "Associations brings on similarities."

There are those with good intentions who intend to win others by fellowship. They insist that good will ultimately come from negative associations. The person with the negative behavior will eventually change. At least, this is what we assume. Occasionally, this may be true; however, this is not the norm. A clean garment doesn't remove the stain from a dirty garment by rubbing against it. On the other hand, when the dirty garment rubs against a clean one, the clean garment usually comes out soiled.

It's better not to let bad associations rub off on you. It's better to be alone than in bad company.

IT'S THE INSIDE THAT COUNTS

But the LORD said unto Samuel, Look not on his countenance, or on the height of his stature; because I have refused him: for the LORD seeth not as man seeth; for man looketh on the outward appearance, but the LORD looketh on the heart.

1 Samuel 16:7

One day, Mama was at a woman's house. The people present were discussing who was going to heaven. Mama was new in the Lord.

One woman said, "My mama said, 'Ain't nobody going to heaven that wears make-up.'"

At the time, Mama was wearing make-up. She went home with tears in her eyes. All this was new to her. She didn't understand. There were so many things said that puzzled her.

That night, Mama prayed, "Lord let me know what counts with You!"

He came to her in a dream. In the dream, she was in a dimly lighted room. There was a body lying on slab of wood. The body was cut vertically into two parts. The intestines were showing. Mama saw the hand of the Lord. She could only see from the wrist down. The hand went over to the body and tilted down from the wrist. It pointed to the inside of the body.

God spoke, "It's the inside that counts!"

"The heavens proclaim the glory of God. The

skies display His craftsmanship"
Psalm 19:1 NLT

Man looks on the outward appearance. God looks at the heart. Man often judges by circumstances. Favor is influenced by social, economic, and political status. Choices are often made based on personal appearance. Financial wealth usually weilds influence. Social acceptance is frequently based on outward appearances. This is not the way that God judges man.

For the word of God is quick, and powerful, and sharper than any twoedged sword, piercing even to the dividing asunder of soul and spirit, and of the joints and marrow, and is a discerner of the thoughts and intents of the heart. Neither is there any creature that is not manifest in His sight: but all things are naked and opened unto the eyes of Him with whom we have to do.
Hebrews 4:12-13

His judgment is divine. His judgment is righteous. God judges us based on the thoughts and intentions of our heart. With Him, the inside counts!

IT'S BETTER TO BE THOUGHT A FOOL

Be not rash with thy mouth, and let not thine heart be hasty to utter any thing before God: for God is in heaven, and thou upon earth: therefore let thy words be few. For a dream cometh through the multitude of business; and a fool's voice is known by multitude of words.
Ecclesiastes 5:2-3

Mama's father would periodically tell her, "It's better to remain silent and be thought a fool, than to speak and remove all doubt."

According to a Welsh Proverb, three things it is best to avoid: a strange dog, a flood, and a man who thinks he is wise.

A Rumanian Proverb says, "There is no wise response to a foolish remark."

A Greek Proverb says, "All things good to know are difficult to learn."

Fools assume that wisdom and knowledge are easily obtained. Both come through much effort. The apprehension of them requires diligence and patience.

On a number of occasions, I have asked Earline to spell a word for me. She is always confident that her spelling is correct. She is also confident of the definition of the word. Over the years, there have been many times when a child in our family was asked to complete an assignment for school. If a dictionary or encyclopedia with this information was not readily available, we would call Earline. She has a history of reading both books. Does this mean that Earline knows everything? No! She has a simple formula.

She will readily tell you, "I never use a word that I don't own. If I don't know the meaning of it, I don't use it. If I don't know how to spell it, I don't use it."

This is a lesson many of us could learn, yet some of us want to impress others with our mastery of the English language. A fool's voice speaks loudest when he attempts to impress others with words that he does not own.

Even a fool, when he holdeth his peace, is counted wise: and he that shutteth his lips is esteemed a man of understanding.
Proverbs 17:28

This is my own proverb, "If you never use a big word, no will no know that you don't own any. If you one incorrectly, the person who owns the word will identify you as an imposter."

It's best to attempt to apprehend wisdom and knowledge. The first step in the process of learning is admitting that you don't know. If you don't say anything, no will know that you don't know. If you try to fake it, you might not make it. It's better to be thought a fool, than to speak and remove all doubt!

In the Midst of Strength There is Weakness

That he told her all his heart, and said unto her, There hath not come a razor upon mine head; for I have been a Nazarite unto God from my mother's womb: if I be shaven, then my strength will go from me, and I shall become weak, and be like any other man.
Judges 16:17

One day, Mama was talking to a woman. The woman was portraying an image of perfection. Her conversation indicated that she was assured of perfection in her relationship with God. As she spoke, God spoke to Mama.

The inner voice whispered, "In the midst of strength there is weakness."

No matter how strong that we think we are we all have need of improvement. None of us has reached a level of perfection. There is room for growth if we are willing to open our hearts to Jesus. We are never so strong or perfect that we don't need help.

And He said unto me, My grace is sufficient for thee: for My strength is made perfect in weakness. Most gladly therefore will I rather glory in my infirmities, that the power of Christ may rest upon me.
2 Corinthians 12:9

Even the Apostle Paul had areas of weakness in his life. Although God mightily used him, there was room for growth. He was highly educated and spoke several languages fluently. He was taught by one the most respected teachers of his day, Gamaliel.

A French Proverb says, "There is a pinch of the madman in every great man."

Mark the perfect man, and behold the upright:
for the end of that man is peace.
Psalm 37:37

In recent months, a number of people have tried to convince me that they have obtained perfection. The very necessity of needing to prove this shatters their theory of perfection. The sun has no need to prove that it a brilliant and hot light. The moon has no need to prove that it illuminates the night. They just do it. No one argues the point.

FOR EVER O LORD

For ever, O LORD, Thy word is settled in heaven. Psalm 119:89

One day, Mama was praying in her bedroom. She was kneeling at the side of the bed. As she prayed, she heard the Lord whisper in her right ear.

He said softly, "For ever, O LORD, Thy word is settled in heaven."

At this time, Mama had never read this scripture in the Bible. After hearing this message, she was sure the scripture was in the Bible. A short time after hearing this verse in her ear, she heard a minister on the radio quote the scripture reference. Hurriedly, she reached for her Bible to locate the verse. She quickly added this scripture to her memory.

We frequently see signs are bumper stickers that read, "God said it! I believe it and that settles it!"

The word of God stands true on its own merit. The truth is not conditional upon our belief. The only prerequisite is the authority of God. Even when we refuse to acknowledge the truth of His word, His word is settled in heaven.

Recently, I was listening to a CD. It was a recording of songs by the late Bishop G. E. Paterson. Bishop Patterson was the presiding bishop of *The Church of God in Christ.* Although I have had the CD more than a year, it quickly became apparent that I had never listened to one of the CDs in its entirety. It's a two-volume set. One of the songs is entitled, *I Know the Bible is Right.* As the song played, the lyrics quickly captivated my thoughts. In the background, you could hear these words repeated, "I know the Bible is right and somebody's wrong!"

These words will ring true throughout all eternity. Whenever there is a choice between two opinions, the Bible is right. Any error or misconception is on the part of the disagreeing party. God's word has been settled in heaven. That settles it!

REDEEM THE TIMES

See then that ye walk circumspectly, not as fools, but as wise, Redeeming the time, because the days are evil. Wherefore be ye not unwise, but understanding what the will of the Lord is. Ephesians 5:15-17

Years ago, the church would sing a song. In recent years, I haven't heard it. The words said, "Up above my head, I hear music in the air. There must be a God somewhere."

We have names for two of the rooms at Mama's house. One is the *blue room*. This is my former bedroom. The other room is called the *red room*. This is Mama's bedroom. Normally, Mama sleeps in the *red room*. One night, Mama slept in the *blue room*. The next morning, she sat on the side of the bed. Above her head, Mama heard a melody. The words rang out repeatedly, "Redeem the times! Redeem the times!"

Nevertheless they did flatter Him with their mouth, and they lied unto Him with their tongues. For their heart was not right with Him, neither were they stedfast in His covenant. But he, being full of compassion, forgave their iniquity, and destroyed them not: yea, many a time turned he His anger away, and did not stir up all His wrath.
Psalm 78:36-38

On hearing this, Mama became concerned. She wondered if her life was coming to a speedy end. Mama had never read this scripture in the Bible.

And that, knowing the time, that now it is high time to awake out of sleep: for now is our salvation nearer than when we believed. The night is far spent, the day is at hand: let us therefore cast off the works of darkness, and let us put on the armour of light. Let us walk honestly, as in the day; not in rioting and drunkenness, not in chambering and wantonness, not in strife and envying.
Romans 13:11-13

The days are evil and it is imperative that we redeem the times. For years, the world has heard that Jesus is coming back soon. Perhaps, it has been said so long that we have been lulled into a false sense of security. Because the Lord in His mercy has delayed his second coming, some people assume that the delay is indefinite. No matter how long it has been, He's still coming back. He said that He would be back. It's time for us to make preparation for His return. It's time to redeem the times!

Things I Wish my Mother had Taught me

WHOSE CHILD IS IT

In those days they shall say no more, The fathers have eaten a sour grape, and the children's teeth are set on edge. But every one shall die for his own iniquity: every man that eateth the sour grape, his teeth shall be set on edge.
Jeremiah 31:29-30

Whenever a child is acting out, I will often say, "Whose child is it?" In saying this, I am indicating that the child is acting like one of his parents. This is a lesson that I had to learn. It was a painful lesson. Both of my children have different personalities, yet they both act a lot like their mother. One acts more like me than the other one. The traits that they got from me are intensified in both of them.

From the time that I was a young child, I have been told that I look just like my mother. Mama says that if she had a dollar for every time that it has been said, she could have retired a long time ago. While, I may look like her, I don't always act like her. Mama can be more of a suffering servant. While every now and then, I'm the one with the whip clearing the temple. Mama might suffer in silence, indefinitely. On the other hand, I will take a lot of abuse, but sooner or later, an eruption is coming. The longer that it takes the eruption to occur, the greater that eruption will be.

Mama was working on a job. Her supervisor was verbally abusive. Before finally telling me, Mama took the abuse for years. She opted not to tell my sister anything. I had other plans. I shared the information with my sister. For months, I let the abuse go without getting involved.

One day, the supervisor went too far. She told my mother, "Get your little self over there and sit down in that chair!"

When Mama told me, I tried to hide my anger. I didn't share this information with my sister until much later. My mind was made up. This treatment had gone far enough.

The next morning, I called the chief executive officer of the company. I told her how my mother was being treated.

Shocked by this information, she said, "The other day, I asked Ms. Russell how things were going. She has never given me any indication that anything is wrong."

I responded, "You didn't ask her the right question. She's not going to complain. She doesn't know that I am calling and she would be really upset if she did. You have to get her to look you straight in the face. She never looks directly at anyone. When she's looking directly at you, ask her if Ms. Jones mistreats her."

When Mama came home that evening, she told me that she had been called to the office. As Mama told me what had happened at work, my face remained calm. It was weeks, before she figured out that I had made the call. Every day, she was pondering what had happened. Finally, one day, she asked me if I had anything to do with the abuse being reported. Reluctantly, I told her that I had made the telephone call.

My mother prefers routine activities. She is skeptical about learning anything new. That's not how I operate. There are very few things that I'm hesitant to learn. It's rare that I back down from a new challenge.

My behavior had to come from somewhere. Since, I never knew my father; I can't blame it on him. I just know that it wasn't Mama. The same holds true for my sister. She is not like my mother. Oddly if there is any similarity to my mother in our family, it's my son, Herman.

He likes to go the extreme with people. Herman never looks for the negative in anyone. If it pops out at him, he refuses to discuss it.

When Herman and Earline were both attending colleges in the Atlanta, it was a very interesting time. It was also a very trying time for me. My children are very different. Earline is more reserved and serious. Herman is adventurous and daring. He is a lot like his mother in those areas. He is also charming and he has never met a stranger.

My children were living in Athens, Georgia. On the days when they attended classes in Atlanta, they would park at one of the train stations. They would take the trains to their respective schools. Earline was in law school at Georgia State University. Herman was sixteen and working toward an undergraduate degree at Georgia Perimeter College.

One day, a homeless woman got on the train with them. At least, that's how she identified herself.

In a pitiful voice, she said, "Last night all the homeless shelters were full and I didn't have anywhere to sleep. Can you give me something to help?"

Earline didn't fall for the scam. Herman reached in his pocket and gave her five dollars. Since he wasn't working, this was a big sacrifice. He shared what Earline had given him.

The next day, they were on the bus again. A woman got on the bus with them. She proceeded to talk to the passengers.

In a pitiful voice, she said, "Last night all the homeless shelters were full and I didn't have anywhere to sleep. Can you give me something to help?"

Herman reached in his pocket and gave her a dollar. Earline was concerned. She didn't want anybody taking advantage of her younger brother.

Troubled, she warned, "Herman that's the same lady from yesterday!"

He responded, "I know! That's why I only gave her a dollar."

This is common behavior for Herman. It's not what I would have done. Nevertheless, it's exactly what Mother Russell would have done. She frequently calls Herman her son.

SOME THINGS ONCE GIVEN CAN NEVER BE RECLAIMED

Howbeit he would not hearken unto her voice: but, being stronger than she, forced her, and lay with her. Then Amnon hated her exceedingly; so that the hatred wherewith he hated her was greater than the love wherewith he had loved her. And Amnon said unto her, Arise, be gone. And she said unto him, There is no cause: this evil in sending me away is greater than the other that thou didst unto me.
2 Samuel 13:14-16

I never had the opportunity to wear white on my wedding day, but I wish that I had. For one of my weddings, I did wear off white. It hardly meant pure. I never got to go the prom, but I wish that I had. I did get to go to many nightclubs. I never got to enjoy growing up, but I wish that I had. I did get to watch my baby grow up.

Occasionally, we move too fast. At times, we make decision for all the wrong reasons. Sometimes, we choose all the wrong relationships. Sometimes, we choose all the wrong choices. Sometimes, we give away something that we can never get back.

Some things, you can only give away once. You only get one first time. You only get one first love. You only get one first kiss. You only get one first marriage. You only get one first child. There are times when, the first things don't come first.

When you decide to take the first things out of order, you tamper with order of nature. The things that were meant to be sacred and precious become distasteful memories. Rather than being treasured moments, they become things that we wish we could erase.

Once you give your innocence away, you can never get it back. If you give your virginity away, you can never get it back. If you give your heart away, you never get it back.

NEVER DATE ANYONE YOU WOULDN'T WANT TO MARRY

Did not Solomon king of Israel sin by these things? yet among many nations was there no king like him, who was beloved of his God, and God made him king over all Israel: nevertheless even him did outlandish women cause to sin. Shall we then hearken unto you to do all this great evil, to transgress against our God in marrying strange wives?
Nehemiah 13:26-27

Today, I saw a young woman wearing a T-shirt. The front of the shirt read, "You used to be my type, but I got help." I thought, "Now, that's good... That's a statement worth giving some thought."

Recently, someone said something to me about a young man. I didn't tell them, but within myself, I thought, "He's r-e-a-l-l-y not my type." Nowadays, what is my type? I'll keep that one to myself. Often, it will appear that we don't know our type. What we say we want in a mate and what we choose are often contradictory.

When this happens, we try to transform the person into what we really want. That's providing we have a clear view or perception of our expectations. Anyone who becomes involved in a relationship with expectation of changing the other party is asking for trouble. This trouble is going to be followed by misery.

Wait patiently for the LORD. Be brave and courageous. Yes, wait patiently for the LORD.
Psalm 27:14 NLT

If the person doesn't meet your baseline qualifications, don't get involved in a prolonged conversation. Please, don't spend time in their company when you are vulnerable! I repeat, PLEASE! You can get accustomed to fleas if they hang around you long enough. It doesn't mean that they won't attempt to destroy you.

Know what you are looking for in a relationship. If you set your standards high, be sure to make your qualifications just as high. Don't expect prime rib in exchange for a poor man's steak, bologna. Don't get in a hurry; wait for God to send you prime rib.

IN-LAWS AREN'T REFUNDABLE; THEY DON'T COME WITH WARRANTIES

And he turned unto her by the way, and said,
Go to, I pray thee, let me come in unto thee;
(for he knew not that she was his daughter in
law.) And she said, What wilt thou give me,
that thou mayest come in unto me? And he
said, I will send thee a kid from the flock.
And she said, Wilt thou give me a pledge,
till thou send it?
Genesis 38:16-17

It has repeatedly been said, "I married you! I didn't marry your family."

In theory, this may sound good. In an ideal world, it may even be true. In most cases, it's far from the truth. In-laws come with the marriage. You can move across the country; you can move to a different continent. The in-laws are coming with you. You may not see them in bodily form; nevertheless, they will be there.

The person that you are marrying may seem to have very little in common with their birth family. Trust me; it is there. Somewhere lurking beneath the surface waiting to manifest at the most inopportune time is the spirit of your in-laws. If it doesn't manifest in your spouse, carefully observe your children.

One former pastor would say, "Before you marry someone, you better find out something about the family. You need to know if there is a lunatic in the family. If you think that his sister is ugly, when you give birth to a child that looks just like her, what are you going to do?"

This may seem a bit funny or extreme, but people have a blood connection to their families of origin. Even estranged family members may experience a secret need to be accepted back into the family circle.

God wants all believers to worship together. How much more does He want our families to come together? No matter what has happened in the family's history, we are to work towards unity. Pride and prejudice are enemies of the kingdom. They have no place in the family. We should ask God to give us open hearts towards our in-laws. After all, they are non-refundable.

NEVER DATE ON THE REBOUND; THE BALL WILL KEEP BOUNCING

If . . . you suddenly remember that someone
has something against you, leave your sacrifice
there beside the altar. Go and be
reconciled to that person.
Matthew 5:23-24 NLT

More than once, I have been guilty of this
one. When one relationship ends abruptly, it can
leave you emotionally vulnerable. Your thoughts
are confused and it is easy to make the wrong
decision. At times, a new relationship seems like
a quick fix. You just want the hurt to end. Comfort
in the arms of someone else may give temporary
release; however, baggage from the previous
relationship will follow you into the new
relationship.

Every relationship that ends needs closure.
If there is no closure to the relationship, it is hard
to recover from the loss. Eventually, multiple
wounds may exist. Any wound unattended is apt
to leak. Normally, they leak without notice.

A breakup could temporarily shatter your
self-esteem. If you aren't careful, it may be
destroyed. Disappointment could cause your
vision or outlook to be cloudy. Your perception or
judgment can become faulty. You may settle for a
bad or negative relationship. It may divert you

from your purpose or destiny. Because, the new relationship began under duress, the possibilities of the relationship ending negatively are increased.

Each time, in an effort to stop the hurt, you may lower your standards and requirements. Rather than seeking a more positive outcome for your life, subconsciously you may lower your standards. It could be easy to become trapped in a place where you believe that you just can't do any better. The cycle is in danger of repeating, until you decide to stop the ball from bouncing. Forget about dating on the rebound. It's just not worth the trouble!

A HEART IS PRECIOUS; THERE IS VALUE IN ALLOWING A BROKEN ONE TO HEAL

All of you should be of one mind, full of sympathy toward each other, loving one another with tender hearts and humble minds.
1 Peter 3:8 NLT

I watch a number of reruns on television. I seldom watch prime time television. Recently, my mother and I were watching one the shows that I watch periodically. It has been in syndication for several years. Help often comes in unlikely forms.

On the television show, the star of the program has a radio show. During this segment, a distraught caller called into the radio show. The caller explained to the talk show host the nature of the crisis.

The voice on the other end of the telephone said, "I was in a relationship that ended badly seven months ago. I feel like I'm grieving."

The host responded, "You are grieving. It's not for person with whom, the relationship ended. You're grieving for the dream that has been lost. Allow yourself time to grieve and then move on."

Mama said, "He gave a really good answer."

It was a good answer. It was an accurate answer. Relationships are frequently held together by dreams rather than the reality of the relationship. The best-made plans are subjected to change. Dreams don't always come true. The cliché says that it takes two to tango. It takes two to make a romantic dream come true. When this isn't possible, shake the dust off your feet; sweep the cobwebs from your heart.

But Jesus beheld them, and said unto them,
With men this is impossible; but with God
all things are possible.
Matthew 19:26

Allow your heart to have a brand new start. You've just been through open-heart surgery. After each operation, a trip to the recovery room is necessary. Although the blockage has been extracted, there will be occasional pain. Don't become overly stressed. In time, you will be back on your feet. From time to time, fear will creep in. We are afraid of the process. It may be a slow process, but hold on. If you will trust Him while you wait, God will answer you.

LIFE IS TOO SHORT; DON'T STRETCH THE SMALL STUFF

Man that is born of a woman is of few days, and full of trouble. He cometh forth like a flower, and is cut down: he fleeth also as a shadow, and continueth not.

Job 14:1-2

Sometime ago, I heard someone say, "Don't sweat the small stuff." They went on to say, you could be in a relationship that is ninety-five percent of what you want. That leaves five percent lacking. They further explained that you could become so focused on the five percent that it would begin to outweigh the ninety-five percent.

After becoming consumed by the five percent, you would forget everything that you have. Consequently, you will destroy the ninety-five percent and settle for a relationship that offers five percent. This is my own way of putting it; you give up ninety-five pounds of gold for five pounds of aluminum. In other words, you are *stuck on stupid.*

Life is too short to live in a cycle of continual mistakes. Some things aren't worth the effort. Small things can destroy your happiness and ruin your life. We have to decide what is important and what is just small stuff. We can't allow small problems to escalate into major ones. We can't allow trivial matters to destroy our lives.

I tell you, her sins—and they are many—have been forgiven, so she has showed me much love. But a person who is forgiven little shows only little love.
Luke 7:47 NLT

We have to accept people as they are and where they are. If we expect people to be perfect, we set ourselves up for disappointment. Allow people to make mistakes. When they do, love them enough to forgive them.

It's important to set priorities. Choose your battles carefully. There will be casualties in any battle. Decide if the battle is worth the casualties. Let go of the small stuff. Don't stretch small things into something that it was never meant to be.

THE BEAUTY OF A RAINBOW ONLY APPEARS AFTER THE RAIN

The rainbow shall be in the cloud, and I will look on it to remember everlasting covenant between God and every living creature of all flesh that is on the earth."
Genesis 9:16 NKJ

If I had never known sickness, I couldn't appreciate my health. If I had never known physical weakness, I couldn't appreciate my strength. If I had never known sadness, I couldn't appreciate joy. If I had never cried, I couldn't appreciate laughter. If it had never rained, I couldn't appreciate the sunshine. If I had never known the experience of coldness on a winter night, I wouldn't appreciate a warm summer day. If the rain never stopped, I couldn't see the beauty of the rainbow.

Some pain is designed to refine us. Perhaps, I would never have become involved in prison ministry if I had never gone to prison. Maybe, I would never have reached out to those on welfare, drugs, in crisis, in abusive relationships, incarcerated, and considered hopeless if I had not walked these paths.

The things that we endure are meant to make us better. They are meant to create a heart of compassion. When I wrote my fifth book, *Mama May I*, I got no satisfaction from it. In the process of writing the book, I learned so much. The year before I wrote the book, I wanted to purchase a book that would cover the same issues. If it were left up to me, I would rather have read the book, than to have lived it.

Someone told me, "God knew you could handle it."

That must be true. I lived through the crisis. Today, I see the beauty of a rainbow. It came through my tears.

DON'T WASTE TIME TRYING TO GET OTHERS TO ACCEPT YOU; FIRST ACCEPT YOURSELF

But don't be so concerned about perishable things like food. Spend your energy seeking the eternal life that the Son of Man can give you. For God the Father has given me the seal of His approval.
John 6:27

During the days of my youth, I began smoking marijuana. There was a popular song released in 1969 by The Temptations. It was called *Cloud Nine*. This song describes perfectly where I wanted to be. The lyrics went something like this, "I'm doing fine on cloud nine. Let me tell you 'bout cloud nine... You can be what you want to be... You ain't got no responsibility... Cloud Nine... And every man, every man is free... Cloud nine... You're a million miles from reality. I wanna' stay up higher. I wanna' say I love the life I live, and I'm going to live, the life I love or be on cloud nine... I, I, I, I, I, I'm ridin' high on cloud nine.

That was it exactly! I wanted a life free from responsibility, pain, sadness, and sorrow. I wanted to rise above every circumstance in my life. To put it bluntly, I wanted to be in a constant state of euphoria. I wanted to laugh! At the time, I needed an artificial stimulus to achieve this euphoria. This state of euphoria is often referred to as tripping. When I gave up my marijuana, God gave me the same ability to achieve that euphoria. Only now, I don't need the artificial stimuli. I can trip myself out.

After I finished my undergraduate degree, I worked with a number of programs. On a regular basis, I was required to counsel people in crisis. On one of my jobs, two people asked me why I laugh all the time. One of them asked me if it was because insecurity. Wanting to be professional and fit in, I pondered their comments.

For more than a week, I tried to be deep and serious. Not once did I laugh. One night, as I was washing my hair, the floodgates broke and I began to cry. It seemed the tears would never stop. I cried for every person who had told me about abuse. I cried for every person who told me that they had been raped. I cried for every person who had told me that HIV had infected them. I cried for every person who told me that they had been neglected by their parents. I cried for every person who told me that they were being mistreated by a foster parent. I cried for every sad story that I had ever heard. When I finished crying for all that I just cried.

During this time, I was also enrolled in a graduate program. The next week, I was attending a new class. At registration, the students enrolled in the class were given an introductory package from the professor. Included within the package was a survey. After reviewing it, I decided that it was optional. As such, I chose not to complete it.

A merry heart doeth good like a medicine:
but a broken spirit drieth the bones.
Proverbs 17:22

On the first night of the class, the instructor reviewed the survey. I may have been the only person who didn't complete it. As the instructor began to review the survey, some students were not amused. One question asked, "What type of instructor do you prefer?" One of the answers read, "One who covers the lesson well." After reading this comment, he placed the textbook in the floor and proceeded to jump over the book. He said, "I just covered it." As he continued with the questionnaire, he performed similar tactics.

During the course of the night, we had three or four breaks. When we returned from each break, he had rearranged our chairs. His lecture that night was appropriately termed, *The Power of Laughter*. God did that just for me.

That night, I made a resolution. I made a decree. The decision was unanimous. It was a majority vote. Now, I know that you need more than one person to be a majority. Well, I had that. Me, myself, and I came to an agreement. I will never ever let another human being determine or rule my emotions.

God has given me a gift and I intend to use it. In sickness, I intend to laugh. In sorrow, I intend to laugh. Through trials, I intend to laugh. In joy, I intend to laugh. In the midst of persecution, I intend to laugh. In heartache, I intend to laugh. In the midst of lies being told on me, I intend to laugh. Being abandoned, I intend to laugh. Being persecuted, I intend to laugh.

It may be true that I have only two emotional expressions, tears, and laughter. However, I have a choice. I have made my choice. I chose laughter. I don't need a tranquilizer. I don't need a nerve pill. I don't need a sleeping pill. I don't need drugs. I don't need alcohol. I have a natural high; it's called laughter.

Even in laughter the heart is sorrowful;
and the end of that mirth is heaviness.
Proverbs 14:13

It doesn't mean that I don't feel pain, because I enjoy laughing. It doesn't mean that I don't feel sorrow or sympathy. It doesn't mean that I am out of touch with my emotions. I am very much in touch with them. It means that I look for something funny or positive in every situation. Whenever something shakes me to the point that I can't laugh, I make a concerted effort to get my laughter back. Indeed, there are few things that I can't find a measure of humor in. There is song that says, "After all I've been through, I still have joy." Let me take it a step further, "After all I have been through, I could have lost my mind, but I still have laughter.

"I plead with you to give your bodies to God
because of all He has done for you. Let them
be a living and holy sacrifice—the kind He will

find acceptable. This is truly the way to worship Him" Romans 12:1 NLT

The desire for popularity is normal among teenagers. It is an essential ingredient for a political life. In spite of this, attempts to acquire popularity can create emotional torture. Everyone who pursues acceptance becomes a servant to the pursuit. In order to remain popular, everything has to be done right. You have to say everything right. There's the absolutely perfect look to maintain. Not only do you have to know all the right people, they have to know you.

The greatest drawback to seeking popularity, however, is the weight of trying to give everyone what they want. It has to be given when they want it. There is never an end to the demands. One mistake, one wrong move or tasteless outfit, one wrong word and you're condemned. At some point, we all make mistakes. Real friends love you when you're not perfect. When you make mistakes, they still accept you. They support you in times of trouble. Real friends are rare. If you find one in a lifetime, cherish your friend. Most of all cherish who you are. God created you in His image. Be the best *you* that *you* can be.

Dare to be Different

You will be betrayed even by parents and
brothers, relatives and friends; and they will
put some of you to death.
And you will be hated by
all for My name's sake. But not a
hair of your head shall be lost.
Luke 21:16-18 NKJ

SOMETIMES LOSING MEANS WINNING

"If you try to hang on to your life, you will lose it. But if you give up your life for My sake, you will save it."
Luke 9:24 NLT

Whenever we listen to and obey the Word of God, we are giving up our life to Him. In return, He has promised to give the believer a life greater than anything we could ever visualize. It's a life full of hope, glory, a future, and a wonderfullyexpected end.

In small ways, we are faced with the opportunity to give up our life for Him, each day. Every time you turn off the television to go help with painting the house, every time you refrain from saying something you know that would be embarrassing or harmful, every time you place another person's feelings above your own, you're giving up a little piece of your life.

Every so often, the sacrifices that we are asked to make are greater. Being in the will of God may seem to be inconvenient. There will be times when we are required to relinquish our dreams for a more excellent plan. In attempting to preserve foolish dreams, we frequently hurt ourselves.

Then said Jesus unto His disciples if any man

will come after Me, let him deny himself, and take up His cross, and follow Me. For whosoever will save his life shall lose it: and whosoever will lose his life for My sake shall find it.
Matthew 16:24-25

For each of our lives, God has a perfect plan. We interrupt the flow of His plan by trying to maintain relationships that are not in His plan. This includes personal, business, professional, and family relationships. There will be times when we will need to shake the dust off our feet. When we attempt to maintain relationships that dishonor God, we are attempting to maintain our life. In the process, we lose our life.

The things that God has prepared for us will ultimately provide a more quality filled life. When we relinquish the things that we are afraid to lose, it can be scary. Often, our emotions are clouded. The real fear lies in the thoughts of losing. Everyone wants to be a winner.

What happens when you can't visualize the prize? Rewards are usually reserved for the winner. It is difficult to accept the concept of losing as winning. Who wouldn't exchange a pound of copper for a pound of gold? God's will for our life is gold. Sometimes, we have to lose the copper to get the gold. We have to risk losing that we might win.

CELEBRATE YOUR OWN SUCCESS

So I perceived that nothing is better than
that a man should rejoice in his own works, for
that is his heritage. For who can bring him to
see what will happen after him?
Ecclesiastes 3:22 NKJ

Early in life, I learned never to expect from others what I wouldn't give myself. When I reward myself, it keeps me from being disappointed. Whether it's my birthday or some other holiday if I want something, I'll buy it myself. If it's something that I wouldn't buy for myself, I don't expect anybody else to do it for me.

When I have done a good job, I'll tell myself. If, I'm satisfied with my work, I'm pleased. It's hard to please other people. It's impossible to please people who aren't pleased with themselves.

If their life depended on it, some people wouldn't give you a compliment. They have never received compliments, and they don't believe in giving them. Still others love to receive recognition but never give any recognition.

To avoid all this trouble, I simply compliment my own efforts. Bad news has wings; it spreads quickly. Good news moves at the speed of a turtle. Normally, it fails to reach an appropriate destination.

A Russian Proverb says, "Every peasant is proud of the pond in his village because from it he measures the sea."

Celebrating your own success does not mean becoming arrogant, proud, and boastful. It simply means that when you've done the best that you can, rest in that. If no one ever compliments you on a job well done, compliment yourself. If no one ever encourages you in the midst of discouragement, encourage yourself. If no one ever remembers your birthday, buy your own cake. If you never get a present, buy yourself one. If no one ever appreciates you, appreciate yourself. If no one ever says congratulations, celebrate your own success.

YOU CAN ONLY DREAM FOR YOURSELF

In all labor there is profit,
But chatter leads only to poverty.
Proverbs 14:25 NKJ

Every *real* mother looks into the face of her newborn child and sees purpose, destiny, and promise. I stress real mother because not every woman that gives birth to a child is a mother. Some women serve only as human incubators.

Real mothers dream of their children becoming presidents, kings, queens, lawyers, doctors, and a host of other professions. She sees health, wealth, and prosperity. She doesn't dream of failures, losers, or abusers.

No matter what she dreams, the ultimate reality rests within that child. If the child doesn't see purpose, destiny, and promise, the mother's dreams will never see fruition. A dream has to begin within the child.

Other people will come in our lives. In many of them, we will see purpose, destiny, and promise. We can only dream so far. Just as faith without works is dead, a dream without works is dead. A Japanese Proverb states, "Vision without action is a daydream. Action with without vision is a nightmare."

Go to the ant, thou sluggard; consider her ways, and be wise: Which having no guide,

186

overseer, or ruler, Provideth her meat in the summer, and gathereth her food in the harvest. How long wilt thou sleep, O sluggard? when wilt thou arise out of thy sleep? Yet a little sleep, a little slumber, a little folding of the hands to sleep: So shall thy poverty come as one that travelleth, and thy want as an armed man.
Proverbs 6:6-11

The messages of the world bombard us with negative signals or triggers. They tell us that we need more money, more luxuries, more power, and more things. These things seek to become our heart's desire. There are some who lack the ability and the motivation to make dreams a reality. They say the right things, but there is no follow through. The world offers a quick solution to obtain a measure of success. These quick solutions are often deceptive.

How can we escape these destructive desires? Jesus is the answer. He offers us the ability to make dreams become reality. Plant dreams in the hearts of other, but harvest your own dreams.

SOME HURTS ARE LIKE A VIRUS; THEY HAVE TO RUN THEIR COURSE

She weeps bitterly in the night, Her tears are on her cheeks; Among all her lovers She has none to comfort her. All her friends have dealt treacherously with her; They have become her enemies.
Lamentations 1:2 NKJ

God never promised to protect us from our problems on the earth. Nevertheless, He promises to give us the courage to confront our troubles with His strength. When we find ourselves in a place that is painful or unfamiliar, we want a quick cure. We want the pain to stop and the discomfort to end.

Unfortunately, a quick end to the pain is not the way things traditionally work out. It has been said that time heals all wounds. That statement may not be completely true. Time will make some pains and wounds more tolerable.

Hast thou not known? hast thou not heard, that the everlasting God, the LORD, the Creator of the ends of the earth, fainteth not, neither is weary? there is no searching of His understanding. He giveth power to the

faint; and to them that have no might He increaseth strength. Even the youths shall faint and be weary, and the young men shall utterly fall: But they that wait upon the LORD shall renew their strength; they shall mount up with wings as eagles; they shall run, and not be weary; and they shall walk, and not faint.
Isaiah 40:28-31

There is one requirement in recovering from any trauma. There must be a desire to recover. If the desire is first created in the heart, it will make it easier for manifestation to come. Wait patiently in the process. A pearl of great price is usually created by pain. Consequently, healing has to come by a painful process. Usually, it comes in the process of time.

JESUS REMEMBERS WHEN OTHERS FORGET

O LORD, Thou knowest: remember me, and visit me, and revenge me of my persecutors; take me not away in thy longsuffering: know that for Thy sake I have suffered rebuke. Thy words were found, and I did eat them; and Thy word was unto me the joy and rejoicing of mine heart: for I am called by Thy name, O LORD God of hosts.
Jeremiah 15:15-16

One night, I was sitting at home. It was getting close to midnight. Some emergency made it necessary for me to go to the store. The store was only a couple of blocks away. When I arrived at the store, I bought the single item that I had gone to purchase. When I walked out of the exit door of store, my eyes were immediately directed towards the sky.

What I saw amazed me. The sky was a perfect deep blue. It was a clear night, without a sign of a cloud. The moon provided a brilliant night-light. As I stared into the sky, I was mesmerized. As if they had been painted on a beautiful canvas, the stars were sparkling. As far as I could see in any direction was a perfect picture. It seemed that I saw the sky for the first time. Suddenly, the magnitude of the heavens captivated my thoughts. My thoughts were totally fixated on the view.

God in all His creative genius had created this work of art. He placed the moon in just the right place to provide us light during the night. Each star was held in just the right place. No star violated the space of another one. The sun was held at just the right distance from the earth. There is never a moment when God doesn't know where each of His creations is placed.

From whence come wars and fightings among you? come they not hence, even of your lusts that war in your members? Ye lust, and have not: ye kill, and desire to have, and cannot obtain: ye fight and war, yet ye have not, because ye ask not.
James 4:1-3

This was at a time when our government was actively pursuing Bin Laden and Saddam Hussein. As I stared to the sky, I reminded that God knew exactly where each of them was hiding. He was aware of everything that was happening in Iraq, Afghanistan, and Pakistan. In the midst of all the things that God has to do at one time, He remembered me. In comparison to God's many responsibilities, I seemed so insignificant. In spite of my insignificance, God remembered me! Every time, I was in crisis, He remembered to intervene. He was never too busy to remember me. In the midst of my insignificancy, I was significant to Him.

DON'T DO THE CRIME...

When people do not accept divine guidance,
they run wild. But whoever obeys the law
is joyful. Words alone will not discipline
a servant; the words may be understood,
but they are not heeded.
Proverbs 29:18-19

When we began seminary, we favored one teacher. Mama, Earline, and I began together. During the lectures, he would get so excited. Very often, he would begin to preach. Whenever this happened, he would say, "That's a freebie on the side." This chapter is just that, an added bonus.

Years ago, I would watch some television show the name of which escapes me. Yet, a portion of the theme song stuck with me. "Don't do the crime if you can't do the time."

If you choose to be a professional criminal, there are some rules of engagement. There is a great risk that you will be caught. For some, this will happen soon. For others, it happens later. In anticipation of that devastating day, some things need to be done. Three things are necessities, a lawyer, a bondsman, and a backer.

Although I haven't been arrested since 1986, I still know my bondman's telephone number. The same holds true for my lawyer. Their numbers are etched in my memory. Now, as far as a backer, you need to know somebody with some property. Chances are there will be times when it takes more than money to make bail. Some bonds require property as security.

It is understood that you need a bank. I'm not referring to a commercial bank. I'm referring to funds. While you're rolling in the big bucks, you need to put some money aside for an emergency. It will surely come. I always put money to the side. In addition, don't forget to be generous with those who watch your back! Generosity was what I liked about one of my former associates, Jim. He knew how to spread the wealth.

For which of you, intending to build a tower, sitteth not down first, and counteth the cost, whether he have sufficient to finish it? Lest haply, after he hath laid the foundation, and is not able to finish it, all that behold it begin to mock him, Saying, This man began to build, and was not able to finish.
Luke 14:28-30

Now, how do you serve your time? You have to have a plan. I always had a plan. Sometimes, the plans worked; sometimes, they didn't. One thing for sure, it's best not to go to jail without financial resources. This is not always a possibility. Nevertheless, whenever possible put some money aside for an isolation day. More than likely, there will come a time when you feel as if you're isolated from the world.

Before committing any crime, you need to know the penalty for being caught. When I went to prison, I was roughly able to estimate how much time I would serve of the sentence. Additionally, I knew how much money I would be allowed to spend on a weekly basis while in prison. If I wanted to shop at the prison store each week of my incarceration, there was a minimum amount of money that I needed to take with me. Knowing that the diet provided there would not accommodate my taste buds, I decided to take a small bank (amount of money) with me. When my sentence lasted longer than expected, I had to budget my money to ensure that I was able to shop each week.

When you are down, there is never a guarantee that anyone will send you money. To be clear, the only people that you should expect to send you money are the people who benefited from your exploits. With rare exceptions, they are probably not going to send you anything either.

If you assist a thief, you only hurt yourself. You are sworn to tell the truth, but you dare not testify. Fearing people is a dangerous trap, but trusting the LORD means safety. Many seek the ruler's favor, but justice comes from the LORD.
Proverbs 29:24-26 NLT

When I was doing the *Bonnie and Clyde* thing, my mother refused to take anything from me. Therefore, while I was in prison, she was not obligated to provide for me. Because she loves me, she did it anyway.

Because he hath set his love upon Me, therefore will I deliver him: I will set him on high, because he hath known My name. He shall call upon Me, and I will answer him: I will be with him in trouble; I will deliver him, and honour him.
Psalm 91:14-15

There is one more thing that is worthy of mentioning. I had a fifteen-year sentence! It was not my intention of serving this sentence in its entirety. The best thing that I had going for me (besides Jesus) was a good record. Extending my vacation never entered my thoughts. Why would I want to be in jail inside the prison? While I was there, I didn't get any disciplinary reports. Nowadays, I understand that they charge you in more than one way. In prison, they actually deduct money from your account for disciplinary infractions!

A Maltese Proverb says, "Time gives good advice." Since, I had to be in prison whether I wanted to or not, I decided to make the most of my time. The system needed to give me something back. Therefore, I went to school while I was in prison. There were college credits offered through Massey College. I enrolled in the business program.

If ye fulfil the royal law according to the scripture, Thou shalt love thy neighbour as thyself, ye do well: But if ye have respect to persons, ye commit sin, and are convinced of the law as transgressors.
James 2:8-9

Now, a word about being street-wise, don't try to play a player. A real player knows game. Even an ex-player knows game. You never forget how the game is played. Nobody owes you anything! Be honest and up front. Ask them simply to break you off a piece of change if they can. For the most part, honesty will accomplish more than any game you can play. Whatever they send is a blessing to you. Remember, they didn't benefit from your crimes. When you get out, don't forget to kick back (return) the favor.

A prison is a place where you learn to hide your emotions. You can put them on display for everybody to see if you want to make your time harder. As you are being processed into the penal system, it's best to check your emotions in, too. Don't forget to pick them up when you leave.

Don't Make Settlements That you Can't Keep

And it came to pass, when he saw her, that he rent his clothes, and said, Alas, my daughter! thou hast brought me very low, and thou art one of them that trouble me: for I have opened my mouth unto the LORD, and I cannot go back. And she said unto him, My father if thou hast opened thy mouth unto the LORD, do to me according to that which hath proceeded out of thy mouth; forasmuch as the LORD hath taken vengeance for thee of thine enemies, even of the children of Ammon.
Judges 11:35-36

DON'T INVITE PEOPLE TO EXPLOIT YOU

The poor man is hated even by his own
neighbor, But rich has many friends.
Proverbs 14:20 NKJ

There is an old Kenny Rodgers' song that I sing from time to time. Maybe, sing is not the right word. It's probably more accurate to say that I repeat some of the words. It goes something like this, "You've got to know when to hold them. You've got to know when to fold them. You've got to know when to walk away. You've got know when to fight." I'll add a line of my own; never put all your cards on the table at one time. I'm not referring to playing cards or to gambling. I've never been prone to do either. I'm referring to business transactions.

These are my personal rules of engagement. Know your rights! If in doubt, seek expert opinions, not personal opinions. Well-meaning friends can cause you many problems. The Internet provides a wealth of free knowledge. Take advantage of it. Research everything! Perform research before you hire an expert. Do research to determine if you need to hire an expert. Learn how to negotiate with the experts. Never appear desperate for help! Never ever, tell them (the experts) how much money you're willing to spend. They'll seek more money from you. In the end, you'll agree to compromise more and pay more for the purchase. In the aftermath, the outcome of your situation may be worse than before.

Let not him that is deceived trust in vanity:
for vanity shall be his recompence.
Job 15:31

Be honest in weighing your options. Know what you stand to lose and what you stand to gain. Never ever, take advice from someone who is worse off than you. Don't believe them when they say, "If I were you..." They aren't you. Completely ignore them if they start a sentence with, "I would never..." Right! It means that they already have.

Whether you are considering a major purchase, seeking legal advice or educational advice, information can be found on the Internet. I regularly visit several sites to obtain legal information.

In the state of Georgia, the Governor's Office of Consumer Affairs provides a wealth of knowledge. On more than one occasion, I have contacted them for advice. When the information that is needed falls outside of their jurisdiction, they are usually able to refer you to the right office.

SOME BALLOONS WERE MEANT TO FLY AWAY

By night on my bed I sought him whom my soul loveth: I sought him, but I found him not. I will rise now, and go about the city in the streets, and in the broad ways I will seek him whom my soul loveth: I sought him, but I found him not.
Song of Solomon 3:1-2

There is a time and a season for everything. Sometimes, the season is over. There are things, people, and places that are a part of our life just for a season. With each change of season, we change our wardrobe. There are other things that have to change, too. Living life is not a stagnant process. It requires movement and involvement.

At more than one place of employment, I thought, "This is it! This is the job that I've dreamed of!" It was the place that I planned to retire from. When I was working with welfare reform, I really loved that job. My clients were challenging and there was never a dull day. While I may have made a lasting impression on them, many of them did the same for me. In spite of my intentions, complacency was not meant to be a part of my life. Reality eventually became real. These jobs were only watering holes on my journey through the dessert. The jobs that I loved were meant to fly away.

"Even though the fig trees have no blossoms, and there are no grapes on the vines; even though the olive crop fails, and the fields lie empty and barren; even though the flocks die in the fields, and the cattle barns are empty, yet I will rejoice in the LORD! I will be joyful in the God of my salvation."
Habakkuk 3:17-18

More than once, I have joined a church thinking, "This is it! This church is where I will find the love that will lead to my spiritual growth. This is the place where the love of God is manifested. I'm going to pour everything within me into furthering the ministry of this church." Many of these churches were just watering spots on my journey through a desolate land. Some of these churches were meant to fly away.

More than once, I found *the love of my life*. I use this term loosely. I thought that it was the love of my life. Indeed, heartbreak and pain occurred repeatedly. My wasted tears inevitably dried up. In the aftermath, I have found myself disgusted by someone I thought was the love of my life. I wondered what insanity drove me to involvement in the relationship. Nevertheless, they were only periods of drought, during my travels through places of desolation. They were meant to fly away. For some balloon, I say, "Thank God! They flew away!"

DON'T ALLOW YOUR EMOTIONS (OR HEART) TO GOVERN YOUR CHOICES

For out of the heart proceed evil thoughts,
murders, adulteries, fornications, thefts,
false witness, blasphemies: These are
the things which defile a man:
Matthew 15:19-20a

Some choices are made for all the wrong reasons. They are not made based on logic or reason. Rational thoughts never enter the process. These choices aren't based on Biblical principles or the leading of God. Many negative choices are governed strictly by our emotions.

By pride comes nothing,
But with the well-advised is wisdom.
Proverbs 13:10 NKJ

Pride never seeks wisdom. Pride can be an extremely dangerous guide. More than once, I have been asked how I maintained a negative relationship for an extended period of time. Numerous times, someone has asserted, "You must have really loved him." They were referring to one or more of the men in my past. In most instances, love was not the determining factor. Pride was the culprit. Not willing to appear a failure at anything caused me to continue the disastrous relationship.

Passion can also be a cruel taskmaster. In this instance, I'm not referring to the passion that is confused with lust. This reference is referring to what is termed *the heat of passion* or *the heat of the moment.* A rash decision could change your life forever. In these moments, words are sometimes spoken that are irreversible. Many children have lasting scars from words spoken by their parents in haste. The scars may be invisible on the outside, but the wound is deep within.

His own iniquities shall take the wicked himself, and he shall be holden with the cords of his sins. He shall die without instruction; and in the greatness of his folly he shall go astray.
Proverbs 5:22-23

Anger and rage are also deadly destroyers. They are twin brothers who work closely together. It could be difficult if not impossible to distinguish the work of one from the other. They create chaos wherever they appear. They wreak havoc on everyone graced by their presence. Anger is regularly followed by conviction, condemnation, and regret.

The lofty looks of man shall be humbled, and the haughtiness of men shall be bowed down, and the LORD alone shall be exalted in that

day. For the day of the LORD of hosts shall be upon every one that is proud and lofty, and upon every one that is lifted up; and he shall be brought low.
Isaiah 1:11-12

Take a second look before you leap. Never rush to make a judgment. Avoid hasty decisions. Positive displays of emotional expression can be healthy. They can provide encouragement and healing. Nevertheless, emotions should never guide our choices. If they are allowed to do so, they may destroy our lives.

A Heart is Fragile; be Careful who you Allow to Handle it

"This is real love. It is not that we loved God, but that He loved us and sent his Son as a sacrifice to take away our sins."
1 John 4:10 NLT

Epilogue

A gift is as a precious stone in the eyes of
him that hath it: whithersoever it
turneth, it prospereth.
Proverbs 17:8

A mother is a rare treasure. She is a pearl of great price. Bearing a child does make a female a mother. A mother loves at all time. She nurtures her children, all the days of her life.

As friction and discomfort develop a pearl, a mother's wisdom is developed in the same manner. The things that she suffers will assist her in becoming strong and wise. That is provided she chose the route that leads to strength and wisdom.

A mother's heart bleeds each time her children make wrong decision or choices. While she watches with excited expectation as her children grow, she fears the thought of releasing them into a world that is often callous and cold.

Only one day a year is designated to honor mothers. In spite of this, her struggles begin before the child is ever born. She learns during the birthing process to attempt to control the pain that may ensue throughout the years.

The child that she gives life to may become her greatest source of grief. The child may be her harshest critic, her greatest abuser, and the source of most of her tears. Still, she remains a mother, loving the loveless.

Again, the kingdom of heaven is like unto a merchant man, seeking goodly pearls: Who, when he had found one pearl of great price, went and sold all that he had, and bought it.
MATTHEW 13:45-46

A mother is a rare pearl that developed through suffering! If only we would learn to appreciate the true splendor of her beauty, wisdom.

Other Titles
By
Dr. Charlotte Russell Johnson

ISBN 0974189308   ISBN 0974189316   ISBN 0974189324

ISBN 0974189332   ISBN 0974179340   ISBN 0974189359

ISBN 0974189369   ISBN 0974189375   ISBN 0974189383

Reaching Beyond, Inc.
www.charlotterjohnson.com

Helping hurting humanity to reach beyond the barriers in their life, one barrier at a time.

ORDER FORM

Know someone else in crisis, or in need of encouragement order additional copies of this book to sow seeds of healing grace.

Postal Orders:

Reaching Beyond, Inc.
P. O. Box 12364
Columbus, GA 31917-2364
(706) 573-5942
Email us at: admin@charlotterjohnson.com
Please send the following book(s).

Qty.	Title	
_____	*A Journey to Hell and Back*	$14.95 each
_____	*The Flip Side*	$15.95 each
_____	*Daddy's Hugs*	$12.95 each
_____	*Grace Under Fire*	$14.95 each
_____	*Mama May I*	$14.95 each
_____	*Mama's Pearls*	$14.95 each
_____	*Breaking the Curse*	$14.95 each
_____	*Kissin' Hell Goodbye*	$14.95 each
_____	*Oil for the Wounded*	$14.95 each

Sales tax:
   Please add 7% for books shipped to GA addresses.
Shipment:
   Book rate $3.50 for the first book and $1.75 for each additional book.

www.ingramcontent.com/pod-product-compliance
Lightning Source LLC
LaVergne TN
LVHW051512080426
835509LV00017B/2038